'My birthday wish for ACW is that many budding writers will benefit from the memories, experiences, wisdom, practical advice, compassion, spirituality and sheer humanity of this book. If you sense a yearning or a calling to write, then it all starts here.'

James Catford, patron of ACW, chair of the SPCK Group

WRITE WELL

A Handbook for Christian Writers

Compiled by Amy Scott Robinson

Edited by Amy Scott Robinson,
Jane Brocklehurst, Jane Walters,
Rosemary Johnson

instant
apostle

First published in Great Britain in 2021

Instant Apostle
104 The Drive
Rickmansworth
Herts
WD3 4DU

Every effort has been made to seek permission to use copyright material reproduced in this book. The publisher apologises for those cases where permission might not have been sought and, if notified, will formally seek permission at the earliest opportunity.

The views and opinions expressed in this work are those of the author and do not necessarily reflect the views and opinions of the publisher.

British Library Cataloguing-in-Publication Data

A catalogue record for this book is available from the British Library.

This book and all other Instant Apostle books are available from Instant Apostle:

Website: www.instantapostle.com

Email: info@instantapostle.com

ISBN 978-1-912726-45-5

Printed in Great Britain.

Contents

Introduction

Amy Scott Robinson

The aim of the Association of Christian Writers (ACW) is to encourage, equip and inspire. It aims to do this not just for its 700 members, writers at every level and in many genres, but also, through them, for many more hundreds of readers.

If I had to use one word to describe this extraordinary association, it would be 'variety'. Members range from beginners just exploring the idea of putting pen to paper, to accomplished authors with dozens of published books to their names. There are writers of sermons, picture books, crime fiction, non-fiction; there are faithful scribblers of weekly parish newsletters, and authors who have spent years on one novel. Yet in all this variety, there is extraordinary unity: for the faith shared by all of ACW's many writers, whether or not it is explicit in their work, links all of their lives and is a seed for friendships, support, generosity and a genuine desire for the success of others that is not found in any other writers' association I have ever come across.

With those aims in mind, for its fiftieth anniversary, the ACW offers you fifty essays written across its membership, forming a handbook for any Christian writer, and a celebration of the wonderful group that is the ACW.

The essays are arranged into three sections as follows:

Digging the Well

Ten essays celebrate the founding and development of the ACW, tracing it from long-standing members' early memories of its roots to the encouraging words of its youngest member.

Priming the Pump

This is the 'equipment' section: twenty essays by ACW's experts across the trade explore everything from advice on publishing down to the nitty-gritty of writing in various genres. Whether you're hoping for step-by-step instructions on writing devotionals, or help deciding where to send your manuscript, this section has the practical advice you need from people with knowledge and experience.

Filling the Bucket

The twenty essays in this section were the result of a request put out across the membership for stories of members' writing journeys: their involvement with ACW, the trials and joys of writing as a Christian, the tales of how they started and where they are now. It was difficult to select only twenty of the inspiring tales that poured in, and among them we found words of encouragement, advice, empathy and faith. In this section, you can get alongside other writers, find out what makes them tick and see how many paths there are to using your writing in God's kingdom.

Section One

Digging the Well

Connectivity Matters

Fiona Lloyd, ACW chair

In my filing cabinet, I have a letter dated 22nd September 2004. 'Dear Fiona,' it reads, 'I am pleased to let you know that your entry to this competition has been successful...' Why have I kept a letter that is almost twenty years old? Well, on this occasion it's not down to a lack of decluttering on my part. Rather, this was my first-ever published piece, a short story which had been selected to appear in an anthology.

The reason I'm sharing this reminiscence is that the anthology in question was *Write the Vision*, published by ACW in 2005. Unsurprisingly, while I've had plenty of other items published since then, this particular piece of writing will always have a special place in my memories. And now here I am, in 2021, writing something to celebrate our fiftieth anniversary and feeling thankful for the part that ACW has played in my own writing journey.

Since joining ACW, I've been encouraged, equipped and inspired by writers' events and through conversations with others. I've learned so much about the craft of writing and have also acquired greater confidence in sharing my words. In addition, I've particularly valued the opportunities to forge new friendships and the way in which interacting with people from a variety of Church traditions has challenged and deepened my faith on a personal level.

The strapline for ACW is 'Encourage, Equip, Inspire', and it's essential that these concepts underpin all we do as an organisation. However, the story of ACW is also built on the stories of individual writers, some of whom feature later on in this book. To fully appreciate the significance of ACW, we need to acknowledge the experiences of our membership. I joined in around 2003, but there are many who have been committed members of the organisation for much longer, and I'm grateful for the faithful service of all those who have gone before me.

For the first ten years or so of my membership I managed to stay in the background, entering the odd competition and occasionally attending writing events. It was through one of these – a writing weekend at Scargill House in honour of ACW's fortieth birthday – that I gradually started to get to know other members and become more involved. In 2014 I joined the committee as membership secretary, before taking on the roles of vice-chair (2016) and subsequently chair (2020).

It has been an immense privilege to serve ACW in this way. I calculate that I've worked alongside around thirty others during my time on the committee, and I'm aware of many others before me who have diligently served in this capacity. The job descriptions and responsibilities may have evolved over the years, but all have been united in their desire to promote good writing and to enable Christians who write to be part of a supportive network.

The current full complement of the committee consists of thirteen members (we also have co-opted members from time to time). Between us, we manage membership applications and renewals, produce a quarterly magazine, organise competitions and writing events, and oversee a network of local writing groups. We also cultivate and maintain relationships with other organisations such as Media Associates International[1] (supporting writers and publishers in countries where Christianity is under attack) and Christian Resources Together[2]

---

[1] littworld.org (accessed 24th March 2021).
[2] www.christianresourcestogether.co.uk (accessed 24th March 2021).

(an umbrella organisation linking publishers, booksellers and writers).

As a committee, we recognise the importance of staying connected. We meet at least three times each year (in addition to writing events), not just for business reasons but also in order to spend time with one another and to pray. This emphasis on being together has been a key feature of the history of ACW.

The organisation began life as the Fellowship of Christian Writers (FCW), initially an informal support network. But the idea tapped into a real need within the Christian community, and so the group steadily grew. In the late nineties, the name was changed to the Association of Christian Writers, and the organisation was registered as a charity. (As an aside, I love how the original name – 'Fellowship' – underlines the importance of connectivity in our development as writers.)

Fifty years is a long time, and ACW has had to change and adapt along the way. My initial membership was confirmed by a small card (now sadly lost) bearing my membership number, and early communications came via the post. Nowadays, most things are done electronically – a massive change for the organisation. However, the advantage of this transformation is that it has widened the scope of ACW, providing extra opportunities to communicate with members via our eNews bulletin and the wonders of social media. In 2020, digital advances meant that we were able to set up virtual writing events for the first time; a new way of meeting and learning together that gave much-needed support during a difficult season.

One of the biggest challenges along the way has been coping with the demands of growing from a small local group into a national organisation, while still retaining the core values of ACW. It's great that ACW now supports Christian writers across the UK (plus a few from overseas), but this has meant adapting processes and means of connection along the way. Previous chairs – I can count at least six during my membership

– have also had to guide the organisation through the rise in self-publishing and deal with the implications of GDPR.

There are plenty of other writing associations out there, but I believe ACW offers something unique in that it provides an intersection between faith, writing and community. It functions at both a national and a local level, meaning that Christians who write can engage with like-minded individuals in a number of different places. A network of local groups gives a safe space for people to share their writing and to support one another in prayer. (My own local group has been great at listening to my rubbishy first drafts and cheering me on.)

At a wider level, the increased use of social media has given our members greater opportunities to connect and to support one another. Sharing triumphs and disappointments with other Christian writers online can help alleviate the isolation and sense of discouragement often associated with writing (whether as a profession or a hobby). And the proliferation of online booksellers – while not without its frustrations – means that members can encourage one another by posting reviews and perhaps sharing them via their own social media accounts.

All those who are keen to take their writing seriously – whether anxious novices or multi-published veterans – share a desire to improve and hone their skills. The second part of the ACW strapline focuses on the importance of equipping members by giving them the tools to develop and refine their writing. ACW writers' days tend to have a particular focus, but often feature advice that can be applied to other areas of writing, too. Further guidance on the craft of writing is shared in our magazine, *Christian Writer* (formerly *Candle & Keyboard*), and via local group meetings. One of the great strengths of ACW as an organisation is that it welcomes writers of all ages and abilities – and then actively assists them to learn and to grow, building connection in the process.

Inspiration is a trickier notion to pin down, but still constitutes a vital part of what we do. One of the most important aspects of this is the chance to connect with likeminded people. Meeting with others at a writing event can provide the impetus to dust off an abandoned piece of work, to start a new one in a similar style or even to try writing in a different genre. Often, words that started off as a writing exercise can acquire a life of their own and provide a renewed sense of direction. Since I joined ACW, I've been inspired to write modern parables, letters to magazines, devotional pieces and pantoum poetry.[3] Not all of these have led to publication, by any means, but each new thing I've tried has helped me evaluate and improve my writing technique.

Some writers find inspiration through our magazine articles, or via opportunities shared on social media. ACW competitions can challenge writers to approach things in a different way and are great for polishing up editing skills, too. Those who get the chance to contribute to our More than Writers blog[4] or have articles accepted for publication in *Christian Writer* can have their creative juices stirred by reading what others have written.

The thread that links all these aspects together – and the one that separates us from other writing organisations – is our faith. As an organisation, we take seriously our mission to encourage, equip and inspire one another, but we do this within the context of our Christian calling. We write first and foremost not to please ourselves or to satisfy our readers but to serve and honour God. Our connection with one another is important, but our connection to God is paramount.

This doesn't mean that we limit ourselves to writing on overtly Christian themes. Nor should we feel obliged to restrict ourselves to a particular tradition or stream of Christian belief. There is a great need for those who can write for the secular market in a way that reflects our faith without being preachy. And listening to the way others pray or articulate their beliefs

---

[3] A poem composed of four-line stanzas in which the second and fourth lines of each serve as the first and third lines of the next. The last line is often the same as the first. A pantoum poem can be any length.
[4] morethanwriters.blogspot.com (accessed 24th March 2021).

can help all of us to think more deeply about our own faith journey.

Connectivity is a key part of this; the Bible uses lots of different phrases for how we are to relate to other people. We are instructed to love, forgive and help one another. Other passages speak of the need to be gentle and gracious. As a Christian writer, I believe that we can grow both individually and together when we take these instructions to heart. My prayer is that ACW will continue to encourage, equip and inspire Christians who write for the next fifty years (and beyond), and that we will do that from a position of recognising that we are all called by God to write for Him.

Fiona Lloyd is chair of the Association of Christian Writers and is the author of The Diary of a (Trying to Be Holy) Mum *(Instant Apostle, 2018). Fiona also writes regularly for* Together *magazine.*

Writers at Scargill

Bridget and Adrian Plass, ACW president

Bridget – ACW 2021

'Who was that man?'

Those unbelievably old enough to remember *The Lone Ranger* TV series from the 1950s will probably recollect the familiar cry of those shielding their eyes from the sun as the masked rider disappeared over the horizon every week. A similarly puzzled cry might have risen into the air from members of the community as ACW visitors departed in their cars to disappear over the horizon (well, down the lane) after their first weekend at Scargill![5]

I honestly think that many assumed the house would be filled by introverted, serious, 'booky' types seeking solitude in obscure corners or taking solitary walks to seek inspiration. No one, maybe including us, could have anticipated the caring, complex, diverse, talented, funny, dynamic bunch of folk who came through the door on that first Friday, to return in their numbers year after year.

'I thought they'd be really quiet types, whispering as if they were in a library,' said one community member, retreating from the cacophony of laughter in the sun room, having witnessed the group extravagantly greeting each other on arrival.

---

[5] Scargill House is a Christian retreat and conference centre in Yorkshire, run by the Scargill Movement: https://scargillmovement.org/ (accessed 30th June 2021).

'I thought they'd be more up themselves,' said another. 'You know – here to show off what they'd written, big egos clashing, that sort of thing.'

How far from the truth. The highlight for Adrian and me, and I suspect for many of those attending, were the sharing sessions on Saturday evening and Sunday morning, not just because of the quality offerings from the more professional writers, but also because of the enthusiastic support for those tentatively sharing what they had written for the first time.

'I thought they'd only be writing kinda Christian stuff,' said another observer, reeling in shock after one of the evening's more outrageous contributions.

'I thought they'd be happy to starve in a garret, and too preoccupied to ever get round to booking,' said someone in admin, bemused by the alacrity with which food was consumed and the fact that each year the house (including all the en suites) were snapped up on the very day bookings were possible.

'I thought all they'd want to talk about was books,' was perhaps the area where preconceptions were most laughably wrong. It is difficult to put into words the depth of support that we have witnessed over the years as family and health problems have been shared, individual projects encouraged and unusually close friendships grown between people who would never have believed they had anything in common.

ACW, truthfully, we have loved being part of your chaos, your laughter, your tears, your wit and (occasionally) your wisdom. All the things we have seen and hopefully will see again one day at Scargill House.

Adrian – ACW and me

I have been given the rather eye-popping title of 'president' on two occasions. The first was in connection with the Bible a Month Club, a Bible Society organisation that asked its members to contribute a minimum of £3 a month to help those who might otherwise have no access to Scripture.

Those who are offered these strikingly vivid titles usually describe the invitation as an 'honour'. At the time I think it was more of a surprise than an honour. At that stage in my life I was agreeing to almost anything that looked as if it might be a good idea, and if being called 'president' of something would help get Bibles to folk – well, why not?

As it happened, any inflated notions I might have had about my worthiness for the role were dispelled by a letter received by the Bible Society shortly after the decision was made public. A lady who was already a member of the club wrote to say that she wished to cancel her contribution precisely because I was about to become president. Her calm, reasonably expressed argument was that, although I probably meant well, my flippant approach to faith and the Church was inappropriate in the context of the serious business of Bible distribution. If her letter had been more of a rant I probably would not have minded so much. It was the 'more in sorrow than anger tone' that depressed me a bit.

However, I survived that early hiccup and enjoyed my years of attachment to the Bible Society. After all, true enthusiasts are fascinating and single-issue enthusiasts are irresistible. I have to say that I do not think I ever felt like a president, but in view of recent events across the Atlantic, words, as T S Eliot might have said, grow slack.

My invitation to become president of the Association of Christian Writers happened many years later, just as I was sadly beginning to think that I would never be a president ever again. By then I think I cared even less about having a title, although I really do need to point out one negative feature that Bible a

Month Club and ACW have in common. It may be a small thing, but it is worth mentioning for some day in the future when a new presidential shortlist is being considered.

There should be a uniform.

It really does not have to be much. Something along the lines of the ones worn by presidents of those small autocratic republics in South America and parts of Africa. A bit of braid. Tasteful gold epaulettes on the shoulders. Large, engraved brass buttons. A smart, peaked officer's cap with a big shiny badge on the front. That is all it would take. Not too much to ask, surely? I won't go on about it.

A more serious difference between the first and second experiences is one of involvement. I echo everything that Bridget said. In recent years, particularly through those annual gatherings at Scargill House, it is quite true that we have formed relationships, some of them very close friendships, with every kind of writer you could imagine, and some I promise you definitely could not.

What might they have in common? As you will have already learned, this is a particularly interesting question because in terms of age, background, approach to life, Christian experience and levels of amateur or professional achievement in the writing world, they really could not be more varied. It has been our pleasure and genuine privilege through conversations, discussions, workshops and performances to learn the nature of the invisible consensus that motivates our brothers and sisters in authorship.

You see it in eyes filled with restrained passion, in courageous journeys to the front to read aloud to others, in the strange mix of pride and humility when something is well received, in the fierce persistence with which some will work on and change, and work on and change, and continue to work on something that is in them and struggling to get out. And therein lies the clue.

Most of the aspiring or successful writers we have met through contact with ACW are on a spectrum that begins with an embryonic hope that the passion within them is worth expressing in words, to a profound and well-evidenced certainty that the game is definitely worth the candle. We love the similarities, and we adore the differences.

Most of all, perhaps, I agree with Bridget that we have been deeply impressed by the way in which writers in general, and ACW writers in particular, look after each other. Mutual assistance and warm encouragement have been and remain dominant features of our gatherings.

What has contact with ACW done for me? Well, leaving aside the provision of a suitable uniform (about which I promise I shall say very little more), it has caused me to dive more deeply into the depths of what writing means to me, and how I actually try to do it, than I ever expected. Talking to others about these things took a lot of digging and sorting. I am not a naturally talented teacher, and my work began thirty years ago like a mushroom, seeming to grow overnight with bewildering speed. Suddenly I was a writer, and I had to get on and write some more books. How? Speaking in workshops and meetings has provided very helpful opportunities for me to at least attempt some analysis of how that happened, and how, on reflection, I can see why some things have worked and some very definitely have not. I have tried to pass on some of those conclusions.

If I had to tug one golden rule out from the rather diverse list of discoveries that accrued, I would certainly say that (in the world of Christian writing especially, and perhaps in any other when I think about it) a need to tell the truth is paramount. As C S Lewis is said to have written, so rightly, those who wish to be original in their writing should give up the search for originality. Instead, tell the truth. Even if a thousand others have written on the same subject, the truth as I have seen and learned it will always be original. An awful lot of nonsense is still spoken in Church circles. We can help to change that.

The Association of Christian Writers has given us and many, many others a great deal. It has been around for fifty years.

Bridget and I hope it will continue for another half century at least – even if I never get my uniform.

Bridget Plass is a writer and speaker who has spent years doing her very best to communicate things about the love of God that will stand a chance of actually helping people. She has four children and (at last) one grandson.

Adrian Plass has been writing and speaking about all things Christian for more than three decades. The mysteries increase, but the appetite remains. He lives in County Durham with his wife and shares (at last) a grandson with her.

Some Early Days in FCW/ACW

Christopher Idle

'Ann carried her tray up the five stairs from the kitchen. This was it. She would go through the door, give Lily and Sylvia their coffees, and Martin would be there, talking to someone. She would keep her eyes down and talk to Sylvia. She came into the room ... She put the tray down on the table and in spite of her resolve, looked around. He was not there.'

Sorry, you will have to do without the context. But when in a different, real group, Marjorie read those words aloud and promptly closed her A4 folder, the whole room erupted into a mixture of laughter and good-natured groans. For thus ended a chapter from her work-in-progress novel; she had built up our expectation of something between secret romance and angry confrontation, and then pulled the rug from under our feet. We would have to wait for a further month or two before the tension was resolved. Or rather, we found it was stretched a bit tantalisingly further.

And the actual dozen ACW members listening hardly had to say a word; their faces said it all.

It is right that these memories begin with my beloved Marjorie, who sadly died in what seems half a lifetime ago (2003), because my own links with FCW/ACW started with her. Her own beginnings have faded from memory, but probably opened up, like so many, with a suggestion from a friend. Wendy Green, perhaps, who hosted a group in Forest Gate?

Decades before and unknown to each other, Marjorie and I had offered snippets for our respective school magazines; unsurprisingly quite different but with one common element: a touch of teenage wit. Even now, as I reread, I can enjoy a smile with my much-younger self and with my wife-to-be.

Then, from the 1960s onwards, since you can't ignore an itch to write, she was contributing news, verse and reviews to parish magazines, a regular column in nationally syndicated insets, Scripture Union notes and children's stories, with two complete booklets and *Joy in the City*, published by Kingsway in 1988. In the 1980s and early 1990s, Marjorie also reviewed more than a hundred books for *The Church of England Newspaper*, with occasional articles and news items.

It was before the birth of FCW (as it was at first) that we learned one important lesson. We both contributed to a long-running feature of weekly 'Christian Comments' in our local paper, the *North Western Evening Mail*. I was then cutting my ministerial teeth as a curate at Barrow-in-Furness, then in Lancashire, now Cumbria. One mini-series by different writers took various Bible characters, with some creative licence. Marjorie's choice was the Samaritan woman at the well from John 4; she chose to tackle it in first-person mode, and led off with, 'My husband came home drunk every night...'

So far, so good; she hadn't bargained for the sub-editor who set her piece out, 'Bible people no.5, by Mrs Marjorie Idle, wife of the curate of St Mark's: "My husband came home drunk every night..."' Well, I expect it kept them reading.

Then came the birth whose jubilee we are celebrating this year. At some point in its first decade, Marjorie must have signed up to the Fellowship; she began to cross London, east to west, to join the monthly group led by Andrew and Juliet Quicke, professors both. When in 1987 they crossed the pond for Virginia, our loss was America's gain. Douglas and Christine Wood were now chair and vice-chair; Janet Hall edited the Newsletter. Marjorie was soon on the committee; among many new friends she spoke of Joan Garwood and Jan Godfrey, and

Marion Stroud and Brenda Courtie who later succeeded the Woods. These names often came up as contributors to the Newsletter, of which in 1986 she found herself the new editor.

In fact, I nearly started this reminiscence by saying, 'I have just spent an evening with Marjorie'; would that be too startling to those who know that she died? But what a delight and salutary re-education, to revisit the still-treasured issues for which she was responsible! In 1994 the magazine would be rebranded as *Candle & Keyboard*. But from the start she would compose her copy and write out everyone else's contributions on her faithful old typewriter (man in repair shop, "Ere, come and 'ave a look at this, Bert; 'aven't seen one of them in years') and only later graduate to a word processor. No computer then; though ironically one does feature, with mixed fortunes, in the story I started with.

After thanking Janet and others, Marjorie's first editorial, typically brief, said, 'I remember my goddaughter's face the first time she tasted ice cream – puzzlement, pain and delight. Like me today, fitting the jigsaw of contents together, the labour of bringing it forth and the delight of serving the Fellowship of Christian Writers in a small way, with the help of God the supreme communicator.'

After that tasty mix of imagery came news of competitions, events, people, congratulations, writing hints, accounts, a noticeboard and directory, all in sixteen pages of A5. The length varied; at least one issue reached twice that size. How good that she kept all these treasures for nine years, as I have done for the next eighteen!

By November 1994 our in-house magazine had its new title, twenty-eight pages with a 'Review Supplement', and 'proper' printing. I quote the now retiring editor: 'And now I bid you farewell … It has been a wonderful eight years of hard work and of change within the Fellowship, almost akin, in its excitement and satisfaction, to my first years of nursing, when diphtheria was eradicated, antibiotics were being discovered and heart surgery was invented. What a privilege to live through that era and this … Thank you for all your contributions and support … I gladly hand over to Juliet Hughes, whom I welcome on page five.'

The first local group I remember was chaired by Marjorie around 1990, in our remote Suffolk rectory, with four as a standard attendance, including Maureen Long. For three reasons, I rarely joined them. First, they seemed to major on short stories; with one exception (read on…) that was not my gift. Second, this was an area (like part-time geriatric nursing) wholly independent of my ministry as rector of our seven small villages. She shared in so much that was parochial, including hospitality, leading meetings, and (uniquely) playing all seven church organs in turn, that she deserved some space away from me physically as well as mentally. And third, I was occupied with two quite different editorial groups concerned with hymns and hymn books.

Marjorie would later contribute brilliant short stories (I speak as one unbiased) for the eye-opening and church-based adult literacy classes, one to one and richly rewarding, which she trained for and then led on our return to inner London.

In this our second spell in SE15 (Peckham), from 1995, we decided that we would offer to lead a new south London group; by then I had fewer parish responsibilities. So here my memories are of a bouncy and happily mixed bunch. Some were absolute beginners; some came, at first, just to listen. At the other end of the scale, one of our stars who cycled over from Fulham was the multitalented Lance Pierson. He could always be relied upon to conclude the evening on a high note and send us all home enriched.

We often found the mix of experience creative in itself; of course, the ACW provided specialist help for varied levels (excellent!), but here we sparked one another off in ways that were all the better for being diverse. We tried to be truthful as well as kind (once I was sternly told off for being too long-winded, would you believe? Thank you, John!), but our kindest comments were generally for the newest recruits. I don't think we ever suggested a common theme, as I found later in U3A circles; everyone was keen to share their own particular delights and discoveries.

We explored, lightly and incidentally perhaps, what made a particular item 'Christian'; many contributions were far from churchy, but a moment's thought suggested that the values they represented sprang from a Christian worldview.

One slight problem: sometimes we had to steer the group away from the chosen theme into analysing how well it worked as a piece of writing. One small masterpiece on pigeons ('filthy, flying rats'!) brought up some strongly held views but little comment on style or suitability. More serious, and eventually spelling the end of that time, was the erratic attendance. Marjorie and I came to dread the day before the meeting, when the phone kept ringing with apologies for absence. All had cast-iron excuses: 'I have bought five yoke of oxen,' etc. What – hadn't we all booked the date weeks ahead? But leaders and hosts, themselves inevitably committed, must keep smiling to an unpredictable group; they were just so good, so listenable to – when they showed up.

Did we even issue a brief questionnaire on how to ensure a more consistent turnout? The Newsletter certainly ran one. But if so, ours conformed to Murphy's law on such initiatives; the remedies neatly cancelled each other out. Thus, our meetings were too short or too long, too early or too late, too often or too infrequent, and we needed more chocolate cake – no, I made that one up! As so often, it was the busiest who were most reliable.

Meanwhile, many of us appreciated the writers' days in central London, with guest speakers and a regular slot for poetry. At some point the reading aloud of competition winners came to an end; another small disappointment. But we contributed verse to the annual poetry collections; I used to mark some of my favourites, and the names of Simon Baynes and Evangeline Paterson seemed (narrowly!) to collect the most 'likes'. The earliest one I have (1977) was the third: Joan Fry, Anthony Grist, Martyn Halsall, Joan Rowbottom et al.

One topic emerging from time to time at all levels was the notorious writer's block, which I do believe in without ever having suffered from it. My problem is the opposite: once started, I find it hard to stop. How often I have savaged my beautiful paragraphs to meet the required word count (remember when we had to count the words ourselves?), or even tried the patience of an editor by begging for just a little elasticity!

The one short story I did produce, which gained a 'commended' in a national competition, stopped deliberately on a metaphorical cliff edge; my maximum length was used up anyway, so I didn't have much choice. I offered no neat conclusion. The requested feedback didn't criticise the ending, but called one episode 'unlikely'. Curiously, that was a scene I didn't invent but took from real life! But later I found myself wondering what happened next to the missionary nurse who twice escaped murder, and the young widower she somehow found courage to renew contact with, by phone... So I had to resurrect my unfinished tale and sit down at this keyboard, tapping away in order to discover what they did about it. Now my story is twice the length, and I know how it ends.

So here is another unpublished gem, like the book by Marjorie which I started with. Sadly, she never quite tied up all the loose ends before succumbing to the vicious brain tumour that ended her earthly days. One early article had celebrated St Christopher's Hospice in Sydenham, from whose City Ward she herself was to depart in the peace of Christ. I think our grandchildren, most of whom she never knew, may one day enjoy her stories, and learn a bit more about their paternal grandma. And when ACW celebrates another ten, twenty or fifty years, they will know where and how to find the electronically automated membership forms.

Born in Bromley in 1938, Christopher Idle studied at Oxford and Bristol before ordination (C of E) in 1965. He served both urban and rural parishes, retiring at 65 but continuing with hymn-writing, jogging and supporting Barrow AFC. His wife Marjorie, also a writer, died in 2003. Chris lives in Herne Hill and has four married sons and twelve grandchildren.

Ready Writers for Jesus Christ

Caroline Gill
(with recollections from Ready Writer leaders in
South Wales)

I might not have heard about the Fellowship of Christian Writers if David, my archaeologist husband, and I had not been visiting my parents, Timothy and Arlette Dudley-Smith, in their Norfolk home on the same afternoon as Christopher and Marjorie Idle. My father and Christopher are both hymn-writers and have been friends for many years. Christopher served as rector to seven Suffolk parishes from 1989 to 1995, and it was during this time that our paths crossed.

By 1989 I had been living in Cambridge for about a year. I had completed a short WEA[6] course in Creative Writing on Tyneside, prior to my move south with David, who had accepted a post in the Department of Antiquities at the Fitzwilliam Museum.

When I met Marjorie Idle in Norfolk, we fell happily into conversation, during the course of which she told me about her book, *Joy in the City*. Marjorie mentioned the Fellowship of Christian Writers and encouraged me to join. At a time when my rheumatoid arthritis prevented me from travelling to events, *Candle & Keyboard*, the Fellowship's newsletter-cum-magazine, kept me in touch with other followers of Jesus who wanted to

---

[6] Workers' Educational Association, www.wea.org.uk (accessed 22nd March 2021).

write. The Fellowship later became the Association of Christian Writers (ACW). *Candle & Keyboard* developed into *Christian Writer*.

David was appointed to a lectureship at Swansea University in 1992, so we moved to Wales. I was excited to discover that Swansea was designated 'City of Literature' for 1995.

Some years later, David and I met the Reverend Dr Joel Lewis and his wife, Pauline, in Porthcawl. Pauline, who had been 'introduced to ACW by a friend', shares some memories:

> Knowing God was calling me to write, I joined and devoured the magazine, following all the advice and entering anything going.

Joel and Pauline contacted Joan Lewis, a lecturer in creative writing, through ACW. Joan had the vision to arrange the first South Wales writers' day. It was held in a church hall, and participants brought packed lunches.

Pauline continues:

> My husband, Joel, suggested that if we had a good venue and a cooked meal, we might get better attendance (on future occasions).

Thereafter the writers' day took place at The Rest, a hotel and convalescent home on the cliffs at Porthcawl, and became an annual fixture. Joan led the initial event in the new venue, and spoke about writing our stories. *Wings of the Morning*, Pauline's story, was published as a result. Writers' day reports were printed in *Candle & Keyboard*. An account in the February 1998 edition states that Pauline 'recalled the instruction to Habakkuk … to write the vision, and make it plain' (see Habakkuk 2:2, KJV).

Some of the South Wales writers requested more frequent meetings, so Porthcawl Ready Writers was born. The group, named after the words in Psalm 45:1 (KJV), met in Joel and

Pauline's house. David and I joined the growing number of members in the late 1990s.

Pauline adds:

> The problem of space in our home was eased when those who travelled from a distance gradually decided to form their own groups. However, we continued to come together for our annual writers' day, with excellent speakers, often supplied by ACW, with between thirty and forty in attendance.

We struggled to continue our annual event when The Rest was closed down; but with hospitality from a Cardiff church, and now Hope Chapel in Porthcawl, we have been able to gather together until this past year (2020) of COVID-19.

Our little group of Porthcawl Ready Writers remains active. No longer recognised as an official group, ours is a warm and ongoing fellowship. We continue in our various avenues of writing and encouragement. I have moved into sheltered accommodation, and a few of us hope to meet in my 'Eagle's Nest', as I have named my apartment, once lockdown is over.

The new groups that emerged over time were based in Llantrisant, Swansea, the Blackwood area and Cardiff. Patricia Stowell, who went on to set up the Cardiff group in 2010, offers some recollections:

> As a new writer I was fortunate enough to join Llantrisant Ready Writers. I learned so much from its members, particularly Judith and Peter Sly, who ran the group in their home. But because of their ill health and other commitments, I agreed to form Cardiff Ready Writers, which met in our church hall once a month. Here we learned about different genres, enjoyed fellowship together and, above all, sought to bring glory to our Lord through our writing.
>
> We were a diverse group with every member contributing in some way to help each other hone our

skills and appreciate different forms of writing. With non-believing members joining us, it soon became clear that God was using the group as a means of reaching out to others. This gave us an unexpected means of sharing the gospel.

During this time we hosted two of the annual South Wales writers' days, the first in 2014, led by the Reverend Andy Christofides of St Mellons Baptist Church, who was on the editorial board of the *Evangelical Magazine*. Two years later, Christopher Idle led the writers' day, and encouraged us to write from verses of Scripture, perhaps to commemorate special occasions. We were delighted that Graham Oakes, leader of Croeso Ready Writers, could lead us in singing to the praise of our Saviour.

However, because of failing health and ageing, Cardiff Ready Writers disbanded in 2017.

Graham Oakes attended the Llantrisant group until Croeso Ready Writers was launched under his leadership in October 2004. He had a venue in mind as he was a director and trustee of a charity known as Croeso Christian Bookshop and Coffee Shop. Graham looks back on his introduction to ACW:

A friend encouraged me to enter a hymn-writing competition. I entered and forgot all about it until I was informed that I had been shortlisted and was invited to attend the judging at the AGM in London. The top three entries would be put to music and performed on the day. It was a most memorable experience and the first time I actually admitted, publicly, to being a writer.

So began many happy years sharing fellowship with the South Wales Ready Writers, and especially at our wonderful annual writers' days held in The Rest.

As for my song, 'What a Word!': it received a 'Highly Commended' from judge Christopher Idle, who spoke warmly about its theme and structure.

David and I stepped out in faith, forming Swansea Ready Writers (often known as RWS) in about 2004. Meetings were conducted in our home in what I hope was a welcoming, but relatively organised, manner. We began with a time of devotion. Minutes were read out and news was shared before we turned to our prearranged theme. Each evening ended with coffee, tea and conversation.

Sue Williams, one of the founding members, later went on to lead the Swansea group. Sue recounts some memories of her own:

> For me, one of the most enjoyable aspects of RWS over the years was the variety of the people who came along. Although they all had a Christian faith in common, they were very different, coming from a range of ages, backgrounds (both church and career), writing experience and interests. This always made for stimulating conversation and interaction during our meetings.
>
> The types of writing were also extremely varied, ranging through poetry, articles, novels, non-fiction and children's stories to fantasy and science fiction. This gave us all a fascinating opportunity to listen to readings from genres we might never have read for ourselves.
>
> Some RWS members were regularly published authors, and their experience of the publishing world was invaluable for those of us less far along that particular path. Indeed, we were privileged to witness the birth of a ghostwritten biography by one of the group, from the initial idea, through writes and rewrites to the final published volume. Hugely exciting and encouraging!
>
> As a group, RWS regularly attended the annual writers' days in Porthcawl, and the same blend of variety, infectious enthusiasm and inspiration was always evident at those.

Our Swansea numbers began to grow. Sister Marian Thomas, who was already a member of ACW, did not attend our gatherings in person, but supported us through a faithful ministry of prayer.

I was coping with ulcers on my ankles in 2004 and was finding it hard to secure suitable orthopaedic shoes from the hospital. I had read about patients affected by leprosy who had ulcerous feet as a result of injury and an impaired sense of pain. The Leprosy Mission (TLM) was distributing special sandals to alleviate this situation. David and I suggested to our members that RWS might support this cause by holding a writing competition for the Ready Writer groups, with a view to producing a small advent anthology of poetry and prose which could be sold at a launch event.

Christopher Idle agreed to be our guest judge and to write a foreword to our publication, which we called *Christ Comes*. I recall a flurry of emails from a TLM staff member who covered the story in the mission's newsletter. We arranged a prize-giving and at least three launches.

As RWS continued to expand, we struggled to find enough chairs and parking spaces. Helena Wilkinson, one of our members, offered us a spacious room at Nicholaston House, a Christian retreat and conference centre on the Gower Peninsula. Local preacher and historian Gary Gregor came to speak to us in January 2007 on hymns as poems. In March that year we were joined by Graham Oakes and members of the Croeso group. They presented 'a relaxing evening of readings and songs' under the heading, 'Beautiful Simplicity'.

The RWS Directory for 2007 lists eighteen members who attended meetings and three who participated by email. In July of that year a number of us from the Ready Writers groups attended the 'Time to Write' retreat at Nicholaston House. The garden looked out over the sea and was a haven for dragonflies. I led a haiku workshop with Lilian Davies, one of our members. We encouraged participants to draw inspiration from the beauty of God's creation. Gary Gregor led an expedition to the Gower grave of the notable Welsh poet, Vernon Watkins (1906–67).

Other Ready Writers gatherings at Nicholaston included a writing workshop on 'The Desert' facilitated by David (Gill), who had been struck by the Negev on study trips to Israel.

By 2008 David was preparing for a sabbatical and had a book to write. This seemed the appropriate moment to hand over the leadership of the Swansea group. We continued to be involved, and in 2009 when RWS was invited to provide speakers for the writers' day in Porthcawl, we suggested the Reverend Iain B Hodgins, minister of the Gower Pastorate, and Miss Eleanor Jenkins, author of *A Gander's Tale*. The writers' day theme was 'Write for Your Church Magazine'. Eleanor explained how she had turned her back-page column about the local village gander and his geese into a book of modern-day parables, linked to Bible texts.

I created a blog for RWS. Members shared news of their publications and contributed poems and prose pieces. A post from summer 2009 records that Sue Williams gained First Prize in the *Woman Alive*/ACW 'Article Competition' and that David Gill's words and images were to feature in the 2009 edition of *The Lion Handbook to the Bible*.

Photographs of the RWS Christmas party show members in fancy headgear. A wide-brimmed hat resembles the one worn by Puddleglum, a Marsh-wiggle in *The Silver Chair* by C S Lewis. We give thanks to God for times of fellowship and fun.

David and I moved to Suffolk in 2011. We remain grateful for the opportunities that came our way as Ready Writers to know Christ better and to make Him known.

Caroline Gill, who currently lives in Suffolk, was the first leader, with David, her archaeologist husband, of the ACW-affiliated Swansea Ready Writers group. Caroline, who won first prize in the ZSL Poetry Competition on 'Conservation' (2014) and third prize in the Milestones Competition (judged by Brian Patten, 2017), is the co-author, with John Dotson, of The Holy Place, *a poetry chapbook (The Seventh Quarry*

Press, Wales and Cross-Cultural Communications, New York, 2012). Caroline's first single-authored poetry collection is scheduled for publication in 2021. www.carolinegillpoetry.com

We're All Picked for a Purpose

Merrilyn Williams (aka Mel Menzies),
ACW chair 2009–11

Having received my first rejection slip at the age of fourteen (from *Argosy* magazine, home of *The Darling Buds of May*), and worked, when I left college, as 'amanuensis' for author Paul Gallico (his job description), it was to be some years before my first books were published. This came about when a letter I wrote in 1979 was published in *The Church of England Newspaper*, and another in *The Christian Record*, telling of the isolation I felt in church as a divorcee, and that it appeared that people like myself were a source of embarrassment to other Christians.

After reading it, my best friend, wife of my previous vicar canon Michael Cole, badgered me to broaden my readership. Michael put me in touch with Derek Wood of InterVarsity Press, and although Derek told me *The Tug of Two Loves* (being a Christian married to a non-believer) and *Divorced But Not Defeated* were not books for IVP, he freely critiqued my work until, eventually, they were published in 1984.

This being the days before the internet was available, I received letters from all over the world in response to both the magazine pieces and the books, telling me how my experience resonated with others, and marvelling at my openness. In addition, I had one from a missionary in Nigeria and another from a vicar in Sheffield, thanking me for 'that splendid letter' and acknowledging the need for change. Sadly, there were also one or two highly critical responses, which endorsed my reason for writing them in the first place.

The Fellowship of Christian Writers

Derek then put me in touch with what, at that time, was the Fellowship of Christian Writers, which I joined forthwith. I must confess that, as an introvert, I found the first meeting I attended in a London hotel a somewhat daunting experience. To this day I find mingling in large crowds a great discomfort, though I have no problem in addressing them when engaged as a speaker. Despite this, attendance at an FCW event alerted me to the benefits to be found in convening with those of like mind and shared gifts. As a result, in 1985 I started what I believe to be one of the first regional home groups.

Group meetings

Living as I was in Torbay, this attracted a number of FCW members from all over Devon, including novelist Fay Sampson and historian Roger Steer, author of John Stott's and Hudson Taylor's biographies, among others. Here is what Roger recollects of our meetings.

> Over the years it was good to meet together to read what we had written and listen to comments from other local writers both positive and – just as useful! – negative. All reaction was useful and important but I suppose it is true to say that comments from a professional and successful writer like Fay Sampson, and Merrilyn Williams, the group's founder and published author, were especially valuable.
>
> As a group of Christians meeting with a shared interest, we naturally also encouraged one another in prayer and support as we faced challenges in our writing, personal and family lives. In other words, we both laughed and cried together.

I particularly remember an occasion when we met in my house one afternoon, with Roger Steer leading discussions on the similarities between preaching and writing. Fay said that when researching for one of her books, she had found Wesley's written sermons very 'inaccessible'. Roger spoke about Rowan Williams, whose comments on the King James Bible suggested that they should not always be immediately accessible because a little mystery allows the Holy Spirit to work in a person's mind.

Roger also pointed out that Wesley repeatedly refined his sermons, practising on his servant girl until she understood them, whereas the sermons Fay had found were written to be circulated among lay preachers. We then discussed the difference between the written word that is to be read silently, and that which is written to be read aloud, and Wesley's 'rules' on the simplicity of words. My daughter, Susie, who was staying with me at the time, had joined us and, as a vicar and aspiring writer, she had plenty to contribute to the debate. Living in Wales at the time, and having to preach in both English and Welsh each week, she was very aware of the need to choose her words carefully.

Fay Sampson's memories

I remember a roomful of people – more than twenty, I seem to recall. We used to compare our work in progress and receive helpful feedback. We ranged from well-published authors to beginners, but all were supportive of others. It was good to get reactions from such a wide range of listeners.

One day I particularly remember. A large group of us gathered in your sitting room, Merrilyn, but you were unable to join us because of an urgent deadline. Rather than cancelling the meeting, you graciously allowed us to use your beautiful home without you.

Having by this time remarried and moved house, I had a large lounge in which to meet. At times, however, we would go to one another's homes, and sometimes we would invite expert speakers to join us. On one particularly memorable occasion, Edward England, who was for many years a director at Hodder & Stoughton Publishers (London) before setting up his own literary agency, came and addressed the group in Roger's home in Copplestone.

Don't hide your light

My greatest memory of Edward, however, was when, to my huge embarrassment, he introduced me at a large conference as a 'bestselling author'.

'I'm not,' I babbled, blushing furiously. 'It's the book that's a bestseller.'

'Don't hide your light!' Reverend David Coffey admonished me. 'It's not yours to hide.'

His words hit home as never before. Having been brought up not to boast, I'd never truly digested the reality of letting 'your light shine before others, that they may see your good deeds and glorify your Father in heaven' (Matthew 5:16, NIV).

The book Edward England had referred to was *The Last Mountain: Living with AIDS*. Following publication of a number of my books by Kingsway, Lion and other publishers, James Catford of Hodder & Stoughton had approached me and asked me to write the biography of a young woman who had suffered paralysis as the result of a brain tumour. When *Healed Within* was published, he then asked me to write the story of Phil Godfrey. A young scientist who, as a haemophiliac, was in need of regular transfusions, he had become HIV-positive via contaminated blood, just as he was about to take up a post with the Glaxo Institute for Molecular Biology in Geneva. Eventually he contracted AIDS and died, leaving a wife and young daughter.

Unable to cope with the sorrow, I initially turned down the offer. On reading Phil's diaries, however, I eventually gave in to repeated requests and, at Hodder's expense, travelled to Geneva to do my research. The book reached No 4 in the *Sunday Times* Bestseller List and, inevitably, further offers arrived from Hodder, HarperCollins and other publishers.

Throughout this time, I engaged in numerous speaking engagements all over the country. I was interviewed by Steve Chalke before a live audience of 1,500, as well as on national radio in the BBC's London studios. In addition, I took part in a number of local radio chat shows and phone-ins in both the Plymouth and the Exeter studios, as well as with BBC Radio 5 Live, plus regional BBC programmes including West Midlands, Newcastle and Scotland. On one occasion, Pam Rhodes visited me for an interview, and I appeared on *Songs of Praise*. In addition, I blogged regularly on my website www.melmenzies.co.uk and Ezine Articles, as well as leading writers' workshops at The Hayes, High Leigh, and other centres. As always, the *Christian Writer* magazine was a much-appreciated source of sharing and learning and, when I had time, I contributed the occasional article.

Then, in 1998, owing to personal financial problems, I had to turn down publishers' offers and stop writing books in order to start working as copyright and financial manager of Jubilate Hymns. Still living in Devon, and with directors' meetings to attend in London, which included Bishop Michael Baughen and Canon Michael Saward, plus CCL (Christian Copyright Licensing) meetings abroad, I no longer had time to attend national writers' events for what was now the Association of Christian Writers. Nevertheless, I continued my membership, and maintained leadership of the Torbay and South Devon Group in my house, as well as the book club I'd been asked by my church pastor to lead many years earlier. We also had Christmas celebrations together.

ACW's fortieth anniversary

In 2009, despite the fact that I was still working for Jubilate and was in the midst of life-changing trauma in my family, I conceded to requests to take on the chair of ACW. Adrian Plass was president of the association at the time and, in addition to a national event to celebrate the fortieth anniversary in 2011, I arranged a regional one at the Mint Methodist Church in Exeter. Invitations were sent out far and wide, stating that Veronica Heley, a prolific author and well-known writing tutor, had kindly agreed to speak on the subject of 'I Started in Crime'.

I'm pleased to say that it was a success. Sadly, however, I had to take early retirement as chair, owing to escalating family problems.

Writers' group website in 2020

After fourteen happy years with Jubilate, I retired in 2012 and, in addition to being asked to be a regular contributor to *Relationship Development & Transformation*, I had further books published. The latest, my memoir, *Picked for a Purpose*, was clearly the Lord's timing, given COVID-19 and that it focuses on showing those encountering life-changing difficulties or mental health problems that God is good. He sows seeds in our lives, nourishes them and grows them, and with His care we are all picked for a purpose and can bear fruit for His glory. No misery there! All proceeds are for The Prince's Trust, a charity that has empowered nearly 60,000 young people – again, clearly apposite for our times.[7]

Since then, I have decided to stop writing books in order to concentrate solely on my book club and writers' group. Throughout 2020 we 'met' regularly, via Zoom and continued to critique each other's work and pray together. Shortly before

[7] Read more here: www.melmenzies.co.uk/blog/thomass_story_overcoming_p hysical_and_mental_struggles (accessed 24th March 2021).

the March 2020 lockdown, I had a vision from the Lord, telling me that if I were to set up a website and blog for the writers, we could 'feed the five thousand'. I duly did so, and launched a schedule for them – a discipline with which they seemed pleased – and, in the first nine months we produced more than 100 posts.

Subjects vary from memoirs located in Barbados and Tristan da Cunha to inspiring self-help posts, creative writing and planning a wedding. In addition to those who have signed up to follow our blog, by the end of 2020 we had more than 2,000 views from thirty countries, and are, thus, two-fifths of the way to fulfilling the Lord's promise. If you'd like to take a look and encourage the writers with a 'like', or comment, here is the link: shinealightonlife.wordpress.com. My prayer is that we may all – across the country and worldwide – use the gift of writing that the Lord has given us to shed His light, His love, His joy, peace and trust to all those in need.

With several books published in the 1980s, Mel then had commissions from Hodder & Stoughton, one of which became a Sunday Times Bestseller. *Her latest book, published by Malcolm Down, shows how we are all* Picked For A Purpose, *and is available from www.melmenzies.co.uk.*

A Christian Writer is a Writer

Who's a Christian

Veronica Zundel (member from 1979)

In 1979, when I joined what was then the Fellowship of
Christian Writers, I was new to London and just beginning to
think of myself as a writer. I worked as an office junior at Thirty
Press, publisher of *Crusade* and *Third Way* magazines. Although
my job was essentially admin, opening post and packing parcels,
the editors, knowing that I had a University of Oxford English
degree and had had a couple of features published in *The Baptist
Times*, let me write the odd book or film review as well as helping
the *Third Way* editor with editorial work.

FCW still met in the Kensington (or was it Knightsbridge?)
home of Andrew and Juliet Quicke, for informal meetings of
small numbers of people writing in very different fields. My
main involvement was with its annual poetry competition, run
by the much-missed Evangeline Paterson. I never managed to
win it, though I got the odd third prize and commendation, and
always a poem in its anthology, *Christian Poetry*. Later I joined in
the writers' days when they happened in London, and though
they weren't always relevant to my by then rather specialised
field of writing – Bible reading notes and a magazine column –
it was good to meet up with other writers and indeed with agents
and publishers who knew the opportunities for Christian
writers.

At that point it was an organisation with a very mixed range of abilities and experience among its members; you didn't have to be published to join, and I have to admit that as I got more established, with a non-fiction book or two to my name, I sometimes got frustrated with the frequent focus on beginners and how to write better. I knew I could already write well; what I wanted was guidance on where to place my writing! At times it felt as though the magazine, then called *Candle & Keyboard*, was essentially the same every issue, something that can't be said of the now *Christian Writer*.

It was only with the change of name from Fellowship to Association that ACW began to look like a more professional organisation. By this time, however, I had other commitments in my life (marriage, a child and demanding but also rewarding church involvement) and was less active as a member, though very much still writing. It was only with my first Scargill writers' weekend (which I went to not even realising ACW was involved in the event!), and then with the launch of the More than Writers blog, that I began to get more involved again.

Over the years I have valued the contact with other writers struggling with all the things writers struggle with – rejections, lack of monetary reward, writer's block, finding time to devote to writing – but with the added dimension of being a Christian, seeing one's writing as a calling from God and wanting to write truthfully and ethically. I have needed the constant reminder that being a writer is of value in the kingdom and not a lesser vocation than being a cleric, missionary, doctor or social worker; churches don't always 'get' the life of members working in creative fields.

Writing is a lonely business, especially if you are an extrovert like me and need to get out among people to regain energy for life. To know that one is travelling this path with others is reassuring and encouraging. Even if no one else is doing quite the kind of writing you are doing, there are common issues – yes, and common joys too (what can beat the thrill of first seeing, touching, smelling a pristine new book with your name on the cover?).

Being rather an addict to joining organisations, and also having had a breakdown, a baby and two bouts of cancer in the last twenty-five plus years, I haven't been as able to contribute to the life of ACW as I might have liked to. But I'm still grateful for the fact that it's there, and have a respect for it as a body that is constantly aiming to raise the standard of writing by Christians, both for the Christian market and for the wider world.

A few years ago I rather impulsively enrolled on an MA course in Writing Poetry, run by the Poetry School in London together with Newcastle University. The course took me three years instead of the prescribed two, since just after the first term I was diagnosed with breast cancer for the second time, and having limped through the second term I realised I would have to defer for a year. This meant that I was studying with one cohort in my first year and a completely different one in my second year (with a summer school in between where I didn't really belong to either group).

I was struck by the fact that in my first year group there were four acknowledged Christians in a group of eleven, and in my second year group at least three out of twelve (counting myself). I'm not aware that any of them belonged to or had even heard of the ACW, and to my shame it didn't occur to me to mention it. Perhaps, if they had heard of it, they thought of it as a body for people who did some mysterious thing called 'Christian writing', wholly different from ordinary writing? It is a hard image to shake off, especially for those of us who mainly write, as I do, specifically for Christians.

Yet I suspect the vast majority of members are writing for the general market, and if and when their faith shows up in their writing, it is often not explicitly having Christian characters in their novels or putting an evangelistic speech into the mouth of one of them. Rather, our faith permeates our writing as it permeates our lives, by influencing the choices we make and the sort of person we are becoming or aspiring to become. It is far bigger than not including swear words or illicit sex in our fiction. (Come to that, there is a great deal of illicit sex in the Bible and quite a few swear words, though they're rarely translated as such. I often say that if the Bible were published for the first time today, Christians would want to ban it for its heady mix of religion, sex and violence!)

I believe we need to extend the definition of 'Christian writer' (and, indeed, 'Christian fiction') so that it embraces Graham Greene, Susan Howatch, Tim Winton, Jon McGregor (all of them confessing Christians); the social commentator Malcolm Gladwell, rediscovering his Mennonite roots – even possibly my favourite living novelist, Jane Gardam, who while not publicly Christian, treats faith with both sympathy and humour in her novels and is the mistress of the redemptive ending. We need to find role models for our writing not just in each other, helpful though that is, but in those whom the world acknowledges as great writers, and who somehow in their writing make God visible while never preaching or enforcing conversion on their characters or indeed readers.

Let's not dismiss writers like the wonderful Catherine Fox (whose first novel was published by Penguin, no less) just because she portrays explicitly Christian characters (mostly clergy!) as flawed, sinning and often wavering in their faith. She is a hugely accomplished writer, but her career path illustrates the pitfalls of being a Christian and a writer and attempting to meld the two: her writing journey has been stalled not just by an extended period of writer's block, but by the fact that her work was too Christian for the general market and too raunchy and honest for the Christian market.

For myself, I don't think any of my work except perhaps my poetry is going to break into the big wide world beyond the Church (though in 1983 I did, to my great surprise, win the Best Specialist Columnist award at the inaugural Magazine Publishing Awards, beating columnists from the *Mail on Sunday* into second and third places). I believe I have been called to write for the faithful, and after all, if all the good writers go out into the wide world, the Christian market will be left with the not-so-good writers, which isn't ideal.

But I do want to say, let's be even more ambitious about our work than we already are. The change from Fellowship, which implies mutual support in our writing journey, to Association, which implies a professional body, marked a determination to write well enough to compete with writers whose work graces the shelves of general bookshops and even supermarkets and airports, to write well enough to win prizes and be reviewed in the broadsheets. I think as a body we are still a long way from that, and most of us won't attain it (as indeed most writers don't, Christian or not). But if we don't aim high, we will only ever hit low. Read the Booker list and other prize-winners; read the best literature in both fiction and non-fiction; especially read those whom you suspect of having a Christian faith, whether it's explicit in their work or not. Don't be afraid of reading material that contradicts your values: 'the one who is in you is greater than the one who is in the world' (1 John 4:4, NIV). Read the Bible as literature, in big chunks, and notice how skilfully it tells its stories and how little authorial comment is necessary. Read, mark and learn. Then go and attempt to do likewise.

And here endeth the sermon for today.

Veronica Zundel is a freelance non-fiction writer and poet who now has her state pension but doesn't plan to retire from writing. She blogs at www.reversedstandard.com and www.princeodoemena.com/articles

ACW Through the Year

Eleanor Watkins (member from the late 1970s)

I first saw something called the Fellowship of Christian Writers mentioned in a Christian magazine, probably the *Christian Herald*, sometime in the late 1970s. I'd already had a handful of children's books published by Victory Press, but had no contact at all with other writers, and only very briefly by post with publishers and editors. I thought I'd like to know more, and discovered there were meetings held in London, so duly signed up, left my young family of three boys and travelled to the capital from the depths of the Welsh borders. It's a four-hour journey, so I stayed the night before and eagerly turned up at the given address, a large imposing townhouse, somewhere, I think, near Victoria. So keen was I not to be late that I was the first to arrive, and was warmly welcomed by a lovely gracious lady called Olive Ayres, one of those people who seem to exude the love of Jesus.

The room soon filled up, the speakers arrived, and I was hooked. I loved the buzz, the focus on books and writing, the new people I met. Our hosts, Andrew and Juliet Quicke, had recently ghostwritten Jackie Pullinger's inspiring story of her work with drug addicts in Hong Kong;[8] copies were available and I was able to get mine signed by the authors. Much later I

---

[8] Jackie Pullinger with Andrew Quicke, *Chasing the Dragon* (Hodder & Stoughton, 1980).

lent that copy to someone; it wasn't returned, but years later turned up in a box of donations at the bookshop I helped run, so I still have it. That first ACW day was a good one for me.

Sometime afterwards, the venue moved to 84 Margaret Street, handy for the Oxford Street tube station. I think they were also at Euston Road, NW1, for a while. Numbers had increased; so had the variety of speakers and the topics they covered. Friendships were begun, many of which grew and flourished and remain to this day. We picked each other's brains, shared one another's experiences and gleaned valuable knowledge from publishers, editors, booksellers and fellow authors. The word 'networking' was not used as widely then, but that is what we did. We networked, and we loved it.

I was enthralled by speakers of the calibre of Adrian Plass, Evangeline Paterson, Michael Farley (who later lived in our town and ran a poetry group that I joined), Noreen Riols and many others. When chatting over lunch and coffee breaks, it was reassuring to find them very 'normal' human beings and not on some higher plane as I'd imagined. At one writers' day I found myself queuing for the loo next to Veronica Zundel, whose magazine articles I had long read and admired for their unconventional and bold viewpoints. She wore a red sweater dress, and chatting to her I was relieved to find her quite a 'normal' person too!

There was a debate in FCW at one time about whether non-Christian writers should be invited as speakers – I'm so glad they went for it. We were greatly enriched and inspired by them. I remember being in a workshop with William Horwood, author of *Duncton Wood* and other series, and being very encouraged when he critiqued my contribution in a positive way.

One particular meeting stands out for me. I had been going through changes and struggles in my spiritual life, which resulted in a new and joyful experience of being filled with the Holy Spirit. Every day, it seemed, the Lord was giving me opportunities to be a channel of His blessing, and I went to the writers' day that weekend convinced that I was to be used in some special way. I have a good (often overactive) imagination, and had visions of someone collapsing, me praying over them and the person being miraculously restored!

At every coffee and toilet stop on the way, I was on the lookout for that person or situation in need of my input. Nothing showed up. We stayed overnight; I headed to ACW while my husband and daughter went off to London Zoo.

The room was already buzzing with conversation. I saw some people I knew and made a beeline for them. Then I noticed a small, slim, red-haired lady sitting quite alone in the middle of rows of empty seats. I knew immediately this was the person, so I went over and asked if I could sit with her. She shyly said I could, and told me she'd never been before and didn't know anyone. I fetched coffee and we exchanged pleasantries. And then the floodgates opened and she poured out her heart: the tragic loss of her three-year-old daughter from a rare and terrible genetic illness that meant she could not have more children, how her husband had lost his faith and she was struggling. All day long, at breaks and lunch, we talked. Her name was Brenda Benton. She told me she wrote poetry and would love to go up and talk to the speaker, Evangeline Paterson, but lacked the confidence. After a bit of encouragement, she did approach Evangeline, had a good chat and came back glowing.

That was the start of a friendship that has grown and lasted through the decades. Brenda and I don't meet or even communicate often, but we are there for one another. I've watched her regain her confidence, find renewed faith, join a new church and begin to read her poems and speak in public. She joined Aglow International,[9] where she eventually became a leader and travelled all over the country and internationally on speaking tours, and is now a leading authority on the Turin shroud. She has blessed me in so many ways, my little miracle lady.

---

[9] www.aglow.org (accessed 24th March 2021).

For a while I lost contact with ACW. We adopted a little girl, started a local Christian bookshop/coffee shop, were involved in other groups and led a busy life. I still received news from time to time through the newsletter but that was all. By then, there were regional groups dotted about, and when I heard of a new one in the Birmingham area, my interest was revived. It was to be run in the home of Fay Sampson in Selly Oak. Although it meant a round trip of 120 miles, it could be managed in a day, so I decided to throw in my lot with them. Fay had previously given me invaluable help with a children's novel I was writing for Lion; she pointed out to me how two strands of the story had meshed in well together for the first two-thirds of the book, and then I'd suddenly 'lost the plot'. It was something I'd never have noticed myself, and it made all the difference.

I very much admired Fay's Pangur Ban series and had read them with my children, so it was lovely to meet with her and make a whole new group of friends. Fay was living in that area because her husband lectured at one of the Selly Oak colleges; she has since returned to her beloved West Country where she is still writing. At that first meeting in her house, I chatted over coffee with a lady, not a Christian, who had accompanied a friend to the meeting. She was an artist, and commented on how supportive and encouraging the writers were to one another. If it had been a group of artists, she said, there'd have been a lot of rivalry. (I'm sure most artists' groups are not like this!) She was interested in reading Christian literature and I offered to send her some books. I've often wondered whether she read them and what she made of them.

It's the same for us writers and our books, I suppose – we launch them out into the world, and it's always a bonus to get feedback, reviews or opinions from readers. That lady was right about one thing, though – there's always a lovely atmosphere of interest, encouragement and support when ACW members get together. Writing can be lonely, and we all need that input.

Later, the group moved to the home of Cathie Bartlam. I went to several writers' days there and especially remember the lovely lunches. The group was called Crossed Nibs, although someone remarked that with the advance of technology it might be more appropriate to call ourselves Slipped Discs!

A spell of health problems prevented me from continuing with the group and I lost touch again for a while. I kept receiving the magazine, though, which had changed from a typed and stapled news sheet to a far more sophisticated layout with a glossy colour cover and larger format, entitled *Candle & Keyboard*. The name change came, I think, around 1993/94. Later it changed format again and became *Christian Writer*. Over the years, it's had some outstanding contributors and has been a rich source of information, inspiration, challenge, encouragement and news. It's kept us up to date with group news, members' successes, editorial needs and publishing trends, and, in later years, ever-changing and developing technology. I met two of the publishers who produce my books directly through the magazine, when they set out the aims and needs in the world of book publishing and asked for submissions. At least nine of my books have come into being from connections made through the magazine, not to mention the friendships that have developed.

And then came the online group, which at some point had changed its name to Association of Christian Writers, and with it came new beginnings, a new aspect, a whole new lease of life. What can I say about the group, apart from that it's possibly the best thing since sliced bread? With the setting up of ACW online came new levels of communication; suddenly, people who were just names on paper or on book covers became real people, real flesh-and-blood human beings. We learned about each other's families, their homes, jobs, localities, family histories. We shared each other's aspirations, difficulties, struggles, triumphs and tragedies. We rejoiced when others rejoiced and wept when they wept. Of course, the group is mainly about writing, so we share our successes and failures, our disappointments, frustrations, visions and needs. We climb to the mountaintops with one another and sometimes struggle together. Within the group there is another, private, prayer group where deep needs can be shared in confidence. Along with many others, I've never failed to find prayer support, encouragement, practical advice and the strength to press forward. We care for one another, as whole people and not just writers. We love one another. And we have especially valued one another during the time of coronavirus separation and difficulty.

So thank you, ACW, for all you have been, are and will be. Huge thanks and gratitude are due to the hard-working and fantastic committee members and contributors, past and present. You rock! Long may ACW live and grow and flourish, and be a rich source of blessing.

Eleanor Watkins is the author of more than fifty books for children and adults plus numerous short stories and articles, one of the most recent being her childhood memoir Blue Remembered Hills, *published by Onwards and Upwards.*

Fran's Dead Sea Scrolls

Fran Hill (member from 1990)

In our study is a magazine file, stuffed with yellowing sheets of paper. It's my 1990s writing file. They're pre-computer pieces – some handwritten, most typed – and I view them as my personal Dead Sea Scrolls. There are poems, sketches, flash fiction, flash-in-the-pan fiction, stories, memoirs, scripts, ambitious plans for unambitious novels, a smattering of acceptance letters, and rejections enough to paper the study itself. One spurned radio script bears a producer's rude, thick-black capitalised message: NO!

The file also contains evidence of my early involvement with the Association of Christian Writers, or, as it was, the Fellowship of Christian Writers.

In September 1990, my youngest of three skipped off to infant school near our house in Hampton, west London. The next day, I enrolled on a creative writing course, determined to improve on previous efforts. Until then, my oeuvre had featured angst-filled teenage poems about unrequited love, existential despair and the Bay City Rollers, plus comic poems comprising insults about friends and family with which I joyfully spoiled birthdays and anniversaries.

I'd also ripped off revered Christian songs and choruses.

It was time to grow my writing up.

I started attending FCW London gatherings at some point in the early 1990s, abandoning husband and children for the Shepperton line train up to Waterloo. The London writers' days were held at various church premises. Names and locations of the churches elude me, as do names and faces of people I met, although I do remember custard creams during the breaks. If I met you at a writers' day, then – particularly if I swore undying friendship and allegiance – forgive me.

Being part of a fellowship of Christian writers was hugely affirming and I secured my first official writing 'gig' in 1997: a feature article for the *Christian Herald*, a national Christian newspaper. Several features followed, then Russ Bravo, the editor, agreed to let me loose on the back page, writing a regular humour column about life as a Christian and churchgoer. Fortunately, Andy Robb's 'Derek the Cleric' cartoon appeared underneath it. Readers often told me, 'I turn to Derek first, and then I read your column while I'm there.' It wasn't exactly praise but you take what you can get.

I began to write for *Woman Alive* and other Christian magazines. *Woman Alive* commissioned me to interview the late Roy Castle's widow, Fiona, and ghostwrite her chapter in the anthology *Encouraging Women*. Dressed in my mumsy cardigan, I spent an afternoon at Fiona's elegant home and learned what a cafetière was. Then, as a newly trained English teacher embarking on my second career, I pitched to what was the *Times Educational Supplement* – now *TES* magazine – the national for the education sector. I was to write a monthly opinion column for five years as well as other features, quizzes and reviews.

I was cheered on in all these early ventures by my local group led by Donald Burling in Isleworth. A scrap of paper in The Scrolls says I led a workshop for this group in 1998 on 'Writing for Publication'. As I'd only started in August 1997, this probably counted as fraud, but the authorities seem to have overlooked it and I remain a free and grateful woman.

I committed further offences: the (now) ACW committee asked me to edit the organisation's magazine. I said an impulsive, flattered 'yes' but after seventeen consecutive sleepless nights reneged on the deal which everyone had thought sealed. I wasn't excommunicated as I deserved, although, at the next London AGM, on my table the custard creams had been replaced by rich teas.

The Scrolls also tell me that in March 1999, ACW invited the poet Stewart Henderson to judge a poetry slam competition. I performed a poem in the voice of a lonely woman's diary. Stewart awarded me first prize, despite the fact that I had set it in Sheen near Richmond upon Thames but on a whim recited it in a Yorkshire accent.

One ACW opportunity resulted in both celebration and disaster. In 1999, ACW partnered with HarperCollins in a writing competition. I came second with a chapter from a childhood memoir and the prize – a meeting with an editor from HC – happened during an ACW London event. The heavily pregnant editor I met was keen to publish my book and promised to write to begin negotiations.

However, also that year, I'd received an award from the examination board, AQA. I'd sat English A level as a mature student and beaten the nation's teenagers to the top mark in the UK. The national press covered the story and I took my family to the award ceremony. At the celebration buffet, to which interested parties had been invited, I was arguing with my nine-year-old daughter about excesses of chocolate cake when a man approached. 'I'm from Michael Joseph Publishers,' he said. 'We're interested in your story. Are you writing a book?'

As green as Kermit where publishing was concerned, I said, ssshing my whining child, 'That's kind of you, but I am already talking to a publisher.' He wandered away to talk to others not welded to smeared offspring.

Have you guessed? The following week, I heard from HarperCollins. The editor keen on my story was on maternity leave and her replacement did not 'feel so passionate' about it.

I'd tell you I hadn't eaten chocolate cake since but that would be a brazen lie merely for comic effect and a neat, cyclical structure for my anecdote.

My new teaching career left no time for Saturday gallivanting or local ACW meetings. I took a break from membership and rejoined once our children had flown the nest. By then, we'd relocated to Leamington Spa, my birthplace.

In 2013, I unearthed a Leamington-based ACW group, established in 2009 by Margaret Bowdler. It meets four times a year on Saturdays. Not all the members are local and several travel more than forty miles (in non-COVID times) wielding notebooks and packed lunches. I coordinated the group for several years before handing over the reins to someone sensible: Heather Flack. I derive huge enjoyment and cheer from my ACW 'tribe' and count them as friends. We draw heavily on collective group expertise for workshops, advice and encouragement. We've tried all sorts of writing – historical fiction, poetry, humour, fantasy – surprising ourselves with our genre-bending abilities and with what we can write in half an hour flat while simultaneously cramming our faces with cookies or cake.

Technology has transformed the ACW and its member experience. Back in the 1990s, we used the mail, the phone and pigeons. Now, the ACW Facebook page offers daily conversations and the prize of a teacup by your name if you start enough off. The More than Writers blog site gets a daily visit from me and I've written for it on and off, and off and on, currently off. I'm on the ACW Twitterati rota which means juggling two Twitter feeds at once. I have to watch that I'm not reposting self-promotion from my own Twitter feed on the ACW feed; I'd look like an egotist, when as everyone knows, I'm truly the world's most humble person.

I met Tony Collins, guru of the Christian publishing world, at an annual writers' retreat weekend run by ACW president Adrian Plass and his wife, Bridget, at Scargill House. Many ACW members attend and go home half a stone heavier but inspired. The house is set high among the sheep-dotted hills and dry-stone walled lanes of the Dales: if you listen carefully, you can hear the *All Creatures Great and Small* theme tune as you approach. During one retreat, Tony suggested I write a memoir about the teaching life, something like James Herriot's but without the barns, pork pies and messy birth scenes. We decided a diary format would suit the story and, two years later, SPCK released *Miss, What Does Incomprehensible Mean?* – 2020's least hashtaggable title – on to an innocent public.

My launch team comprised ACW members Deborah Jenkins, Ruth Leigh and Georgie Tennant. We dubbed the book 'Incomp' and the team 'The Incomps' as we all ran out of patience saying the full title. Their support in prayer, squillions of messages and banter has been precious and hilarious during the Valley of the Shadow of Dearth of Promotional Opportunities experience that characterised launching in lockdown. On a wider level, so many in ACW gave support as I launched 'Incomp'. They read it, reviewed it, shared and cared, and I paid no one more than £500.

As a non-driver, I've travelled to ACW writers' days in London, Bath, Derby and Birmingham via train, on buses, in taxis and, sometimes, in other people's cars. One memorable journey was – I think – to Bath with ACW local friend Philip Davies, a mild-mannered ex-vicar who writes for children and young people but drives as though he's in the emergency services. A short course of tranquillisers restored my equilibrium but not, alas, his reputation.

The days are always a treat: the reunions, the bookstall, the speakers, the workshops, the Drink-Your-Weight-in-Coffee challenges. Memorable presentations include Nick Page speaking on the craft of writing in 2013 in Birmingham. My notebook says, 'Eat cake!' Was this Nick's writing advice or just imprudent self-talk? Andy Seed, a primary teacher and writer, said in 2014 (Derby?) that, in written dialogue, what is not said is as important as what is said, and that has influenced me since, as well as making my characters sound evasive and dissembling. In 2020, a 'non-hug' ACW day saw Mark Faithfull presenting on public speaking and promoting one's wares. His advice that 'it's not about you but about what you can do for your audience' flipped my thinking.

ACW writers' days – both national and local – necessarily transferred to Zoom during the 2020 and 2021 lockdowns. I was privileged to speak at the first Zoom national day in July 2020, presenting on the 'small things' and how we should not despise them. The prophet Zechariah attended, thanks to Zoom, which transcends boundaries of time and space, and he was clearly inspired by my talk, as evidenced by the fourth chapter of his book, verse 10.

ACW has brought me and taught me so much. It's been a game changer. However, there's always more to learn and I clearly need to stop using clichés such as 'game changer'.

Fran Hill is a writer and teacher from Warwickshire whose latest book is a funny teacher-memoir called Miss, What Does Incomprehensible Mean?, *published by SPCK.*

Keeping ACW in the Family

Simon Baynes and Lucy Rycroft (two
generations of ACW members)

Simon joined the Fellowship of Christian Writers in its early days. He was a missionary in Japan, so was not able to go to meetings, but he enjoyed the magazine, which in those days was called *Candle & Keyboard*. He even designed a logo, with the letter FCW on keys, and a candle. He still has a leather bookmark, celebrating the silver jubilee in 1996, with that logo on it.

Lucy remembers that logo and was aware of her dad being involved in something called FCW, and later ACW, as she grew up. She even remembers him complaining about the change from Fellowship to Association! Simon would get up early each morning to write (largely poetry), and Lucy remembers him attending writers' days and local group meetings too. But writing was very much something Dad did – none of the rest of the family considered themselves 'writers', although all have ended up doing quite a bit of writing in different ways: letters, sermons, articles, poems to celebrate birthdays and other big events.

Simon came back to England in 1980, so was then able to go to meetings, and he also joined the reading group 'Pilgrim Pens'. In 1989, Lucy remembers the excitement of returning home from holiday to discover that Simon had had a 'yes' from a publisher! His novel, *Jason and Delilah*, was released the following year by Monarch, and Lucy was so proud to have a published author for a father – although it would be several years before she herself were to read it.

Simon became ACW administrator for a few years, and also poetry adviser, and he has enjoyed membership ever since. He was delighted when his daughter developed a gift for writing, published *Redeeming Advent* (Gilead Books Publishing, 2019) and joined ACW.

Throughout Lucy's childhood and teenage years, while Simon was writing alongside leading three churches and taking care of a not-inconsiderable vicarage garden, she was developing an interest in music. Lucy studied it at university, then taught in secondary schools for a few years. Apart from a bit of song-writing, she never considered herself a 'writer'. Parenting, and a break from teaching, gave Lucy the desire to start blogging and connecting with others who might, like her, be trying to pursue their faith in the midst of nappies, tantrums and all-nighters. This led to *Redeeming Advent* and *Deborah and Jael* (Onwards and Upwards, 2020) – but her main writing output, nearly nine years later, is still her blog, The Hope-Filled Family.[10]

For the Silver Jubilee in 1996, Simon wrote a poem, which appeared in *Silver Threads*, a booklet published to celebrate the occasion. This is the poem (with 'twenty-five years' changed to 'fifty'!):

We Will Rejoice
'Autou gar esmen poema – We are his poem', Ephesians 2:10
It is time to rejoice, though the sky seems darker
the road seems rougher than when we began;
we have made our choice: let the world shift round us,
we will raise our banner for God and man.
For fifty years we have kept our faith
we have laughed and prayed; we were younger then.
We believed in the grace and the power of God

---

[10] thehopefilledfamily.com (accessed 24th March 2021).

and through him, the power and grace of the pen.
It is time for a modest celebration
though all we have thought and seen and heard
is from one source only; we acknowledge gladly
we are wholly dependent on the Word.
So let us quietly give thanks to the Maker
for we are his poem; we have made our choice.
We will, though humbly, though well aware
of the darkness, we will, we will rejoice.

Simon Baynes was a missionary in Japan from 1965 to 1980, and then vicar of three churches until 1999, when he retired. Within the ACW he held the roles of administrator and poetry adviser.

Lucy Rycroft is a writer and Christian parenting blogger at thehopefilledfamily.com. She lives in York with her husband and four children.

A Voice of Our Own

Jonathan Bryan (youngest member)

Seven years ago I wouldn't have been able to write this, not because I couldn't physically write (I still can't), but because no one had taught me to read and write. Perhaps knowing I am the youngest member of ACW you are not surprised, but when I tell you I am fifteen and had to be removed from school to be taught basic literacy, you will realise how unusual my story is.

Following a car accident in utero I was born with severe cerebral palsy and a number of life-limiting conditions which have left me with very little control over my body and, in particular, no audible speech or the ability to use my hands for signing or even pressing buttons with accuracy. Based on my outward appearance, I was labelled with profound and multiple learning difficulties (PMLD) on entering special school and given a sensory curriculum. Literacy was reduced to listening to the teacher read an oversized toddler book, showing us the pictures and feeling objects related to the story.

At home, books had become a lifeline to me. For as long as I can remember my mother has read to me. During the days, weeks and months I spent in hospital we curled up together and escaped into other worlds: Giant Country, Narnia and Middle-earth. Through my years of silence, books nourished my mind and prevented mental decay.

By the time I was seven it had become obvious that there was going to be no progression in the literacy instruction at school, beyond some initial playing with letters that might be done at preschool. At home I was listening to *The Hobbit*; at school, our class book was *The Hungry Caterpillar*. So, at the start of Year 3, my mother removed me from special school for a couple of hours a day to teach me phonics, whole-word reading and basic numeracy. The summer before, I had tried out an eye gaze machine which I found frustrating because the machine struggled to read where I was looking. Thankfully, my carers and mother could see where my eyes were pointing, so they stuck words or letters to a Perspex board which they held up between us. Learning to read for myself rather than being reliant on people reading out loud was wonderful. And gradually, through a complicated system of choosing from a selection of words presented to me, I was beginning to form stories of my own. Meanwhile, I had covered a phonics scheme and had progressed to a Perspex board with the alphabet grouped into blocks and colour coded. Selecting a letter on my spelling board involves looking at the group of letters followed by a colour, so for every letter I need to move my eyes twice on the board.

While writing a story I came to realise that when I had a word in mind, it was easier and less frustrating to have a go at writing it, rather than waiting to see if it was a whole-word option presented to me on the board. So I started spelling. Words, phrases, emotions I had held in my head came tumbling out on the page via my eyes. Like a bird freed from a cage, I could now sing in unrestricted landscapes.

Sometimes people find it interesting that it wasn't the desire to chat that unlocked my voice, but a longing to communicate through the power of the written word. Writing is my passion. Through finding the right word, my soul has an expression beyond my internal world of colours, emotions and drumbeats.

At the start of Year 5, aged nine, I had caught up academically with my peers and joined my local primary school, and it was in English during the spring of that year that I was introduced to the depths of poetry. Starting with Blake's 'The Tyger', I wrote a rendition for my tenth birthday, encapsulating my hopes and personality, which left the teaching assistant grabbing a tissue and leaving the room!

I once read somewhere that every artist has one piece that flows from their soul without much preparation or planning. For me that experience happened for one of the first poems I wrote; my speech and language therapist was present for one of her monthly visits and anticipation crackled:

Song of Voice
As adept fingers point
My silent soul emerges,
Like the dawn blackbird's song
Suddenly breaking the black.
Music buried in the mind
Sings melodies divine,
Of ancient tales yet untold
Unfurled to men astound.
Whose beauty hears my voice?
What depths saddened my pathway?
Soaring eagles spread wings
I fly to my destiny.

Yet, all the time I was enjoying the freedom of my voice, I was acutely aware of my friends and the thousands of others labelled with PMLD and not taught to read and write in school.

During the summer of Year 5 I became quite ill and very excited that my time to go back to Jesus' garden had come. When I was young I had been very ill in hospital and had visited Jesus' garden, a wondrously real place I can't wait to live in for ever. In the long and laborious process of getting better, I felt God had given me extra time to make a difference for children like me. As a voice for the voiceless, I began to campaign for all children to be taught to read and write, regardless of their educational label.

Just think for a minute about what being literate means for you. We use literacy for enjoyment, learning, escapism, communication, socialisation, education, empowerment, employment, relaxation, sharing and inclusion. Now imagine also being unable to speak. For us who are non-verbal, being able to read and write is not just a life skill, it is also our voice.

And there is nothing better than being able to communicate using your own words. In the New Testament, Zechariah is made non-verbal by the angel when he doesn't believe that he will have a son; and although he is a priest, his opinion on his son's name is not sought until his wife interjects. Even then the people treat him like he is deaf, by making signs to him despite the fact that he can hear and understand. But it is not until he writes, 'His name is John' (Luke 1:63), that his opinion is taken seriously.

When you are non-verbal, being able to communicate with words also changes people's perception of you. Often people who don't know me approach me in my wheelchair and address me like a pre-verbal toddler, in a higher-pitched voice; I named this degrading tone 'special'. When I reply using my spelling board the pitch drops and the conversation becomes more appropriate for my age.

The dangers of making assumptions based on labels is one of the messages I talk about with my charity Teach Us Too,[11] as we go around universities and schools talking to trainee teachers, professionals and school heads, promoting the idea that all children should be taught to read and write, regardless of their educational label.

After reading my story, one teacher in Cumbria embarked on a literacy journey with all of her PMLD pupils and discovered that not one of them fitted the label of having profound and multiple learning difficulties. Using a variety of methods from eye gaze to raising a hand for 'yes' and 'no', she increased their access to language and discovered that they all not only understood but could also express opinions, ask questions and comment on things. They all found a voice. So

---

[11] www.teachustoo.org.uk (accessed 24th March 2021).

when one of their classmates died, they could all find expression for their grief and the gamut of emotions that accompanied it.

Assisting writers as they discover their literary voice is one of the gifts ACW gives to people like me, starting out on their writing journey. In our society it is becoming increasingly difficult to bring a distinct Christian voice to the media, with the name of Jesus causing particular issues.

When a short children's documentary was made of my life, I requested it followed me for my confirmation and campaign, and relevant footage was gathered. However, when the final film and script came through, my confirmation and any reference to my faith had been erased from the final cut. Long hours of work later I had re-edited the script and managed to convince the editor to include fifteen seconds on my faith, which included the name of Jesus, although they still tried to change this when my friend was in the recording studio reading my words for me.

Naively, I thought that when it came to writing my memoir I would not encounter the same issues. After all, this was to be my story in my words, but again at the final manuscript stage the editor not only erased 'Jesus' and at best replaced His name with a 'higher spiritual being', but for apparent ease of reading also sent the changes as a clean manuscript so I couldn't track the alterations. In a very short deadline I compared the two, and with some difficult conversations with the editor, Jesus made it back in.

As ACW celebrates fifty years, this is a golden opportunity for the organisation to look not only back, but also forward to encouraging, equipping and releasing Christian writers and their distinct voices in an increasingly censored society. As I know from my own life and the work of my charity Teach Us Too, there is an indescribable joy in finding a voice of our own.

Jonathan Bryan is a champion and advocate for literacy education for all children, particularly those who, like him, are non-verbal.

74

Section Two

Priming the Pump

The Hook

(or Catching Your Editor)

Tony Collins

You may have seen film of baby turtles hatching, scrambling out of their sandy nest, making their way down to the edge of the foam, dodging marauding gulls, then braving the first wave, only to become a treat for any roving shark. Perhaps one in a hundred will make it to adulthood.

Books are like baby turtles. A few of the strong and lucky survive. Publishing is evolution in action, if you want to be published by a respected company. You can publish privately, of course, and that is thoroughly worth doing, but it just postpones the winnowing process.

Publishers always have a slush pile awaiting assessment. In a well-ordered publishing house, there will be a discipline of regular review. Most publishers are trying to do far too much with far too little time and even less money, so this discipline is often skipped. I have known proposals simply to be left – ignored, not even glanced at – for months on end. It's management by neglect, of course, and indefensible, but it's commonplace.

Faced with such indifference, an immediate practical step is to ensure you are writing to a person, if the company will allow it. Brass neck helps here. Ring the switchboard and ask for the name of an editor. Sometimes it works. Many companies simply tell you to write to 'submissions': OK, do that, but give it thirty or forty days and then pick up the phone. Keep in mind the parable of the persistent widow in Luke 18.

Some companies outsource their slush pile and will only consider submissions from agents. More on this below.

It is up to you to create momentum and spark curiosity. I have encountered authors who have basically told me, 'I have written the book I wanted to write. If no one wants to read it, that's their loss.' If you are expecting the reader to provide the enthusiasm, you are expecting to fail.

So, what can you do to make your proposal robust and visible? You have to craft a hook.

A good hook is more than something to catch a jaded editor's drowsy eye. It's a reason to buy. Even if your baby turtle makes it as far as the sea, a book faces a lot of competition – not just from other books, but from Netflix and Facebook and *Strictly* and the latest governmental inanity.

A hook will be used by the publisher to catch the attention of bookshop managers and of the media. It will help answer the question: on which shelf would you put this book?

A hook is multifaceted. It includes topic, author and title. It ought to hint at a story, if possible. Even the driest of topics is part of a story, if you look hard enough.

A hook goes to the essence of a book. It will be brief. It should be significant. It might be amusing, or informative. It should create a common thread between writer and reader. Whether you are writing a novel or a 300-word article, you always need a hook. There is an old Fleet Street adage: 'You've shown me the sausage, but where is the sizzle?' A hook always has a sharp point.

Another, less respectful, term is 'clickbait'.

In weighing a proposal, I am always looking for hooks. Here are a few that might grip my attention.

The Archbishop of Canterbury has provided a foreword.

In two years we will celebrate the centenary of …

I had killed six men. I was a hard man, in prison for life.

Last night my wife made me sleep on the sofa.

My gambling habit lost me my home, my job, my wife, my family and my dog.

I have seen two women raised from the dead.

I was Johnny Depp's bodyguard.*

Part of a hook should be the title, and here you need to aim for information and intrigue. Think of your favourite book titles. What makes them distinctive? Many of the titles I have been offered are bland to the point of invisibility. You have to entice, to tantalise, as well as to inform. Often there will be a pleasing balance or tension between title and subtitle. Here are some successful titles:

> *God, Stephen Hawking and the Multiverse: What Hawking said and why it matters*

> *Factfulness: Ten reasons we're wrong about the world – and why things are better than you think*

> *His Needs, Her Needs: Building an affair-proof marriage*

> *The Ruthless Elimination of Hurry: How to stay emotionally healthy and spiritually alive in the chaos of the modern world*

> *God on Mute: Engaging the silence of unanswered prayer*

> *Miss, What Does Incomprehensible Mean?* (Fran Hill's excellent semi-memoir has no subtitle, but a glowing quote by Adrian Plass – 'The Victoria Wood of the classroom' – says everything needful)

The ideal title is both informative and intriguing, holding out the prospect of instruction and pleasure, even excitement. The examples above achieve this goal.

Fiction titles draw much more heavily on shades of allusion. If you are writing a novel, what does it promise? A novel should command attention and imaginative engagement – the capacity to entertain should be part of any author's toolbox – so you can't be too prosaic. A good title arouses a frisson of expectation:

The Handmaid's Tale

A Short History of Tractors in Ukrainian

The Thursday Murder Club

The Spy Who Came in from the Cold

Good fiction proposals sometimes draw on arresting facts to support the novel's premise: during the California Gold Rush the village of San Francisco grew from two hundred in 1846 to 36,000 in 1852; most African slaves were sold into bondage by neighbouring tribes; the last giant aurochs, upon which species an entire ecosystem once depended, was slain in Poland in 1627.

If your novel is light on facts – indeed, if facts have been ruthlessly set to one side – then select an arresting moment to tempt the editor.

A fiction proposal will clearly indicate genre, of course. Provided you are not too ambitious or too flagrant, it is reasonable to suggest comparisons to other novels alongside which your own might stand. Research the list of the publisher you are approaching, to suggest parallels. Avoid the depressingly obvious: for many years every children's fantasy novel was favourably compared to *The Chronicles of Narnia*. (More than a few made it into print, and swiftly out again.)

Every proposal should include a good precis. It takes time, effort and intelligence to summarise a book, but if you skip this step you will probably be ignored. Don't be offended if your wording is not actually used on the cover: your editor has more experience in this area than you do. But your summary is a vital step in the process by which your book wins an editor's sponsorship. Incidentally, you can always tell if an editor has not really grasped the essence of a book, because the cover wording will be too long. Most good blurbs run to a maximum of 200 words, preferably fewer.

The other component in your hook will be yourself. You, the author, are your own brand, and this requires work, more so than ever in these days of slim margins and social media. Wendy H Jones has written eloquently on this, and I refer you to her *Power Packed Book Marketing* (Scott and Lawson, 2016). Every editor will look for information about Twitter followers, friends on Facebook, profile on Instagram, etc. If you have a support base, use it. Whom might you approach for commendations? What articles might you write in support? How well do you interview? Where do you speak? Can you sell your own book? I have worked over the years with many authors who cheerfully purchased 1,000 on publication and came back for more, which is always likely to attract a publisher's attention. (Incidentally, before you sign the contract, make sure you have negotiated a satisfactory author discount. Much easier to agree at the outset.)

A word about devotionals. The Christian literary world is well endowed with devotional material, much of it excellent. I recommend, however, that if you are a relatively unknown writer you do not venture down this path, because the essence of a devotional is that it invites the reader to spend a month or a year in the daily company of the writer. Only a small minority of readers is likely to invest so much time in someone they don't know. Most successful devotionals are written by established authors, who constitute the hook. Devotionals are tricky to summarise well, incidentally.

Finally, you might need the services of an agent. An agent may be more able to push past the guardians blocking the gate, will negotiate a decent contract and keep a watchful eye on royalties and statements to ensure the publisher does what they promised. An agent can also offer guidance on your writing plans and pick out the flaws in your opus. Agents, however, will not waste time on a book without an arresting proposition, an intriguing precis and an author who knows how to present themselves. So you still need that hook.

*Untrue.

Tony Collins has worked for Hodder & Stoughton, Kingsway, Angus Hudson Ltd, Lion Hudson and SPCK, and started the Monarch Books and Lion Fiction imprints. He is now a literary agent.

I Want to Be Published: What Can I Expect?

Alison Hull

Many writers who want to see their books in print assume – or are told – that publishing houses are only interested in established authors. This is not true, either in the Christian world or outside: new authors are a necessity, because even great authors do not live for ever. So if you are looking to be published by a Christian publisher in the traditional way, what do you need to know?

Publishing is a business

If a book does not sell, the publisher loses money. Therefore, they want to take on books that sell. Which means that you, as the author, have to think about the market for your book, from the start. Who will buy it and why? Who is it aimed at? And having identified your market, how are you – and the publisher, because this is a joint effort – going to reach them? How will they know your book is available?

Who publishes books like mine?

This is where you need do some research on the different publishers, and the best place to do that is a good bookshop. If you don't have a good Christian bookshop near you – and I don't – then you need to travel or to go online. And you do need to see who is producing what at the moment. Many publishers have, over the years, given up on certain genres or taken on certain genres, and only looking at what they are doing now will tell you what you need to know.

What you need to find is a publisher who produces the genre of books you want to write; what you do not want, of course, is to find that they have just done a book exactly like yours, or close enough that they will not want another one for a while.

Submission guidelines are not a suggestion

Always research any publisher you are going to approach, by going to their website. You may have got their details out of the *Writers' & Artists' Year Book* (Bloomsbury), but these may be out of date, even in the latest edition. Look at their up-and-coming titles, and not just the ones they have done already, to see if there is an obvious direction of travel. Then look for submission guidelines, and stick to them. No publisher will think you are extra interesting if you ignore these guidelines, or send them a manuscript written in a genre they do not produce.

The submission guidelines will tell you what sort of manuscripts the publisher is looking for, how they want submissions to arrive (by email, by post), what they want – the whole manuscript (see below for writing novels), the first two chapters, just a synopsis. Whatever they require, send it. Make sure you have read it through carefully and, if possible, get someone else to do so as well – our brains often tell us what we think is on the page is there, when it isn't. And remember the selling angle: the publisher needs to know about you as well as your book. Not all publishers ask for media questionnaires, but do tell them if you have a radio slot, lots of followers on Twitter or an active blog with a lot of readers. This is your shop window – tell them everything they need to know.

Having posted this, wait. Do not immediately phone, email or otherwise badger. Leave it six weeks, at least, and then drop them an email. I would suggest sending to just one publisher at a time, starting with the one that you most admire.

Do you need an agent?

For years, on writing courses, I would say to those who wanted to approach Christian publishers that they did not need an agent, and it is true: as far as being noticed, you do not need an agent, and if the publisher states on their website that they will look at unsolicited or unagented material, then you can approach them. But a word of warning: the Christian publishing market has changed. At the very least, when you get to contract stage, getting advice from an agent or from the Society of Authors is now a good idea. It isn't just that contracts can be difficult to understand: publishers will also hold on to the rights to your book, even if they are doing little with them, if you do not ensure your contract is properly worded.

And then?

In the fullness of time, you should get an answer. If it is no, then go to the next publisher on your list. If, however, they express an interest, then you may have to do more writing, produce more chapters, revise your synopsis, complete a media questionnaire… Whatever the publisher wants, make sure the publisher gets, asap, all perfectly checked as before.

What is happening in the publisher's office?

Your commissioning editor, or whoever has expressed an interest in your manuscript, is hoping that this great new idea will appeal to their colleagues. Commissioning editors have targets – they have to commission a certain number of books every year, and those books have to generate a certain amount of money. (Or it has to be believed they will: publishing is, to be honest, simply a huge gamble, but it is one in which a certain amount of information can be relied on. More or less.) So your editor is hoping that your book will not only be another one towards their target, but that it will make lots and lots of money. They have to persuade their colleagues that this will be so. There will be meetings, and more meetings, arguments, projected sales figures: the sales figures of other comparable titles will be considered.

At last!

And for the purpose of this article, all those discussions finally result in success: the publisher wants to produce your book. They are happy to offer you a contract, which will stipulate – or should – a deadline, a word count, and a certain amount of money as an advance. It will also have a lot of other clauses, and this is where advice from an expert is a good idea. There are all sorts of clauses that new authors may not expect, may not understand, or may ignore – don't. The issues are too complex to be explored here, and anyway need to be explored properly. But my advice is, talk to the Society of Authors if you have any concerns, or ask ACW for advice.

Some things, however, are straightforward. You should have discussed word counts, deadlines and advances already, since these are part of the in-house discussion. The length of the book has implications for the price, which therefore affects the profit… you get the picture.

How much?

The first shock for many authors is the advance… not just the fact it is so small, but that so little of it will arrive before you have to write the manuscript. Advances are traditionally split into three, with the first amount being payable on the signature of the contract (ie, you sign the contract, send it back and soon after, the money arrives). The second amount will follow when you send in the completed manuscript and the third will arrive when the book is published. So you will only have a very small amount to keep body and soul in roughly the same place. That is publishing, I am afraid: there are grants out there to help struggling authors, but most need to have other incomes.

The contract is a legal, binding document, so having signed it, you need to stick to it – as does the publisher. Again, if you have been asked for 80,000 words, produce 80,000 words. Do not do what one author did for me, and produce almost twice that number. Do not follow another author of mine and produce a manuscript that bears no relation to the synopsis or chapter breakdown that you submitted in the first place. Do not send the manuscript in late. All these things invalidate the contract, or can do. Very few publishers want to call the whole thing off, but it has been known, and advances then need to be returned.

What happens next?

Contract signed, advance paid, manuscript written and submitted… the editorial process begins. This should be straightforward: your manuscript will be edited, either in-house or by a freelance, or probably by both. The in-house editor will read it to ensure you have written the manuscript you have been contracted to write, and that it hangs together as a coherent whole. They will pass it on to the freelance editor, who will then crawl through it, line by line, to ensure it is the best it can be. Cooperate all you can with both: they want the book to excel.

What if I am writing a novel?

This is slightly outside most of my experience, but novels – particularly debut novels – are often commissioned in a different way from non-fiction. Publishers generally are happy to look at a partly written non-fiction title: so a decision may well be made on just a couple of completed chapters, if the synopsis for the book overall seems to be good. However, novels are not the same as other genres: a great opening chapter can be followed by a weak middle and a feeble ending, so publishers often want to read the entire novel before they decide on publication.

Production

While the manuscript is being written, other things will be happening – the book's cover will be designed and the blurb produced, so that the selling process can begin. All this is done in advance, so the books that publishers hope will sell for next Christmas will be announced to the trade and sold into the shops months in advance. You won't be very involved in this process, except to approve the cover and the blurb. This can be a tricky issue: authors often have a clear idea of what they want their covers to look like, but I am afraid that, if your idea and the company's idea differ that much, you are probably wrong. Book covers are meant to sell – not to tell a story. They need to attract people's attention, and to be able to do so even when they are simply tiny thumbnails on Amazon. Also, as you will realise if you wander around Waterstones, different genres have different 'looks'. So a cosy crime drama will have a very different cover from a Scandi noir title, and a publisher will know all this and will have designers who know what sort of look the book should have. So unless the cover is a complete disaster, you need to accept it.

Publication

Big party, lots of champagne, the press on hand, flash bulbs going… ah, the good old days. If you want any of that, you will probably have to arrange and pay for it yourself. However, don't be too downhearted. I got into publishing just in time to go to a few launches, and they were fun. But often those who turned up, even all fifty of them, expected a free copy of the book as a reward for being there, so while they helped the party atmosphere, they did nothing for sales. However, a good publisher will have a proficient marketing and PR person on hand, and the best (Rhoda Hardie) will have lined up radio interviews and magazine opportunities, if your book lends itself to such things. There are book festivals, local and national: and you should take on the task of doing local PR. If you live in Scotland, you will find that there are organisations to help you. If you don't, there are books – and Alison Baverstock is a good author to look at here.

Alison Hull has worked as a freelance and an in-house commissioning editor, and has commissioned, edited, proofread or been otherwise involved in the production of hundreds of titles.

Writing as a Christian

Anne Booth

My name is Anne Booth, I am a Christian and I am a writer and published author. After university, where I studied English, I had lots of jobs, starting with working in a bookshop for a couple of years, then teaching English in Italy and then studying Pastoral Theology for a year. I am married and we have four children, and while bringing them up I had other jobs, including being a college lecturer, organising art and music in a residential home, and being a carer for my elderly parents for eight years. It is only since 2014 that I have been a published author for children, and I have now had twenty-two children's books published, with a variety of different publishers and illustrators, and translated into different languages. I have written seven picture-book texts, six books for five-to-eight-year-olds, six books for seven-to-nine-year-olds, and three novels for nine-to-twelves. Three more picture books will be published in the next year or so, and I have others on submission and am writing more. My first novel for adults is coming out next year and will be published by Harvill Secker. I am currently working on its sequel, on more picture books, and another novel for children. I work full-time as a professional writer and, thanks to the hard work of my agents, I am managing to earn my living from it.

As a Christian I believe I must pray every day, keep the commandments and, fundamentally, as we learn from Jesus in Luke 10:27, I believe I must try to love God 'with all [my] heart and with all [my] soul and with all [my] strength and with all

[my] mind', and I must try to 'love [my] neighbour as [myself]'. So for me, one of my strengths with which I can serve God, and follow Jesus, is that I can write, and I think Jesus is calling me to do this as a professional author at the moment. I love reading and writing, and I feel incredibly blessed that I am able to earn a living by doing this.

I have only been a published author for the last seven years, but I have been a writer all my life – I started writing stories when I was five.

As a writer I use words to help me work out what I think, and to communicate thoughts and feelings. I write in my private prayer journal. I have written essays for school and university; I write letters and cards to friends and family, to MPs and newspapers; I tweet and post on social media. I have written notices for newsletters. Each time, I try to write to the best of my ability and in the spirit of love. I write letters to comfort or encourage, or just to entertain and cheer. I write prose to work out a truth about a situation, or to advance an argument. I am very proud of a letter I wrote to the local council, which a councillor told me swung the vote and succeeded in getting a much-needed pedestrian crossing put on a busy street. I wrote a letter of complaint to the hospital after my elderly father was treated very badly in A&E, and this resulted in an official change of protocol. I was thanked privately by a nurse for raising the issue, as she said she had been very concerned about what had been happening and dreaded her own mother being brought in, but had been too scared to bring it up. My father received an apology, and the new protocol was brought in to avoid any repetitions. This was a very important piece of writing for me, and was an expression of my Christian faith, using my writing gift to honour my father, to challenge wrongdoing and to speak up for the vulnerable.

One of the pieces of writing I am most proud of was managing to get a letter published in a national newspaper in defence of asylum seekers, and which disagreed with the paper's own anti-asylum-seekers headline! I am still so grateful to God and amazed I got that paper to print it, and I hope God used it to change someone's heart.

So these are all ways I, and all Christian writers, can use the gift of writing, and none of them means that you have to be a published author. If I were to stop being published tomorrow, I could still be a Christian writer, writing to help make the world better, with the Beatitudes in mind. For me at this moment, being a Christian writer does not mean I am called to write specifically Christian material, although I am very grateful to those who help my faith by writing prayer books, or guides, or books on theology and spirituality, or about their own faith experience.

When it comes to Christians being published, I think of the film *Amadeus* and the religious struggle the devout Christian composer Salieri had, when he realised that the very impious Mozart was a far better composer than him. It's important not to have a feeling of entitlement. Being a Christian and a writer does not necessarily make us a good writer, no matter how much we want it to, and nobody in publishing owes us anything. I think that for me, being a professional writer and a Christian is very similar to being a doctor, dancer, engineer, or musician and a Christian, in that whether I am a Christian or not, my faith alone, and my interest in writing, won't necessarily make me good at it. Nobody wants to be treated by a doctor who prays but who doesn't know a knee from an elbow, and writers need to learn their craft too.

If I want to be a professional writer I must respect the genre in which I write. I must work hard. I must read and respect and learn from and support others writing in that genre at this time, and I would also say that this is irrespective of whether they have faith or not – the test is whether their work is good. I have been so inspired by books and illustrations by amazingly talented and creative people who would say they have no faith, but whose words and illustrations are beautiful and full of love, and make the world a kinder and better and happier place. I have no doubt God works through them and I feel honoured to read them and learn from them.

Very importantly, if I am sending out work to be published by traditional publishers in 2021, I must know what else is being published in 2021, and not look down on the market. Personally, I am so grateful to have an agent for my children's books and an agent for my books for adults; I know that they both work very hard to get my books into the hands of publishers, and I listen to their advice. When I am being published I try to be good at being edited, to have integrity and keep true to my vision, but always to behave with respect to those who are editing me, so that we can make the best book we can together. It's a cooperative and rewarding process and it really reminds me of how we all have different gifts. It is lovely and an honour to work with my agents, with designers and editors and marketing and sales and, when I am writing illustrated books, with illustrators.

It may be that you are called to self-publish, and that has a very honourable tradition. The wonderful children's writer Jill Paton Walsh had to self-publish her novel *Knowledge of Angels* and it was nominated for the Booker Prize! I can't go into details about self-publishing because I have no experience of it. For myself I would be daunted by the sheer amount of administration and self-promotion needed, and if I ever were to do it, I would still get professionally edited, as I find the editing process is so important to improve my writing, and also a quick way to learn humility!

Manuscripts are rejected for all sorts of reasons. I still write manuscripts that don't find homes, and that is always hard, but ultimately I just have to mourn for a little and then write some more. I may be, like everyone else, unique in the eyes of God, but in reality, in a crowded market, my books are competing with others that may be similar. For example, I came up with an idea inspired by something I had read in a newspaper a few months earlier, but by the time I mentioned it to my agent, another writer she represents had read the same article and had already written a great book on it! I hadn't written any of it by that time, but other texts I have written and have sent out have been rejected because the publisher already has a similar one.

When I first sent in a children's book, before I had an agent, I had been a bookseller and had MAs in Children's Literature and Creative Writing and had children of my own. I knew lots about children's books and really liked the book I had written, and I was very disappointed when it was rejected. They told me that it was charming, but the pace was too slow, and after talking about it with someone else, I realised that I needed to read more contemporary books, jump straight into the action more, and not linger on descriptions. I realised that my book might well be charming and have been accepted decades earlier, but not in 2012, so if I wanted to be published, I had to learn to write for the current market. That doesn't mean compromising my faith, just being professional. If I am writing a picture book, for example, I have to respect that, in 2021, owing to printing processes, the expense involved in producing the illustrations, publishers' budgets, and the way designers work, it *has* to be within a certain word limit to fit a standard. So I write to that, and I keep reading other picture books so that I really understand how illustrations and words work, and what else is being published at the moment, and can notice where there is a real gap in the market. I can still be myself, and I can ask God to bless what I write and use it, while working within set guidelines. It is actually a fun challenge!

Anne Booth is represented for her children's books by Anne Clark (www.anneclarkliteraryagency.co.uk/anne-booth) and by Jo Unwin (www.jounwin.co.uk/portfolio/anne-booth) for her books for adults.

Giving Up the Day Job

Ben Jeapes

Giving up the day job! Surely the holy grail of every writer! No more make-work, appraisals, office politics, commute to work!

True, but there is… I won't call it a downside. There is a flip side; whether it's up or down depends on your perspective.

I currently make my living primarily from ghostwriting – a task I find very fulfilling as a Christian because it is all about service. I humble myself so that someone else's story can be told. It is not where I thought I would end up; I always meant to be a full-time science fiction writer.

Writing has always been my first love and what I wanted to do. Throughout my working adult career (publishing and technical communications) I had a writing career on the side. I sold my first story in 1990 and my first novel in 1998, and I did my first serious ghostwriting in 2008. None of those paid enough to live off. However, I reached a kind of tipping point where I was picking up work from editors who had previously enjoyed working with me. I diversified from science fiction because editors change genre with their jobs, and therefore so did I.

Then in 2011 I was made redundant, which seemed a good opportunity to develop my freelance career… but no. At that point I had absolutely no work stacked up, just some vague ideas that may or may not have worked. Instead, I took a job that I very soon came to loathe, and was stuck there for the next four years.

This turned out to be a very good thing. The job made it clear I had got as high as I ever would on the greasy pole. It taught me that I am a writer, not on the side, but first and foremost. That is my strength and the only thing I am really good at (though I do possess other skills). It hurt at first but now I'm grateful for the affirmation.

Second, I developed some very good prayer habits just to help me survive the day, relying on God more than ever before for my sheer sanity. I no longer fear for my sanity but I've carried on with the prayer habits.

I also learned self-control. There's a Dilbert cartoon[12] in which one of the characters is in her dressing gown, looking forward to a glorious day of working from home with absolutely nothing to distract her… Until the last frame, where we see that her fridge is taunting her.

Yes, if you're working from home, there's a fridge full of food with your name on it. At my last job, I was within walking distance of a Tesco Express. Even before the disillusion set in, I could see how this might have a downside. However, self-control – as well as being a fruit of the Holy Spirit (Galatians 5:23) – is more than the ability to say 'no'. It is equally the ability to say 'not yet'. I gradually worked my desire to scoff uncontrollably down to rewarding myself with a bag of crisps and a chocolate bar at Friday lunchtime, to celebrate the ending of the week. I managed to keep that good habit when I started working from home.

That's as good a segue as any into the other pluses and minuses of giving up the day job.

When you give up the day job, it's only the 'day' bit you actually give up. You retain the job. Perhaps you can now be much more flexible, able to set your own deadlines, etc. But it is still a job. Would you employ someone who was lazy,

---

[12] www.dilbert.com, 4th October 1997 (accessed 25th March 2021).

disorganised, unreliable? No? Then why should anyone else, if that describes you?

I see a deadline as an outworking of Jesus' command in Matthew 5:37 – let your 'yes' mean yes and your 'no' mean no. If you have said you will meet a deadline, then you will darn well meet that deadline.

In fact, if you have a word count and a deadline, then it's a simple matter of maths to calculate how many words per day you must average between now and then to finish the job. Work it out, factor in weekends and days off, include time for editing and revision, and you will meet that deadline easily. If not – well, see the above point about being organised. You can even put it in a spreadsheet (which is exactly what I do).

In a day job, you can hide in the team. On your own, your shortcomings are thrown into sharp relief and there's no one to carry you. As well as organising your workflow, it is now up to you to handle your accounts, your pension, your taxes and everything else. You now pay for your heating and other overheads during the day – though you can put a percentage of those on your tax return as deductibles. And it is probably up to you to drum up work rather than let it just come to you, so maintaining your website and social media presence is another work overhead that you have to fit around your primary task, which is writing.

(Hint: unless you are a whizz at numbers and/or enjoy this kind of thing, please, get an accountant. You really do not want HMRC one day to start pondering, 'If they are so famous, how come we've never heard of them?' Likewise, while we render unto Caesar what is Caesar's – see Matthew 22:21 – and all that, there is absolutely no point spraying money at Caesar when you can quite legally pay a little less. Caesar will not be the one to point this out to you.)

And then there is knowing when to stop. You will probably be working on more than one project at a time. You could handle them all sequentially, but that probably means you will hone one job to perfection while you develop a very long backlog of other unfinished projects – which will soon shrink to quite a short backlog as clients take their work elsewhere. I divide my day into slices during which I will work on different jobs. Everything gets done a bit at a time, but everything gets done. At 5pm I down tools.

Another characteristic of a job is that it should pay you enough to live off. You wouldn't do your day job for less than a decent working wage, so why should this be any different?

I enjoy the variety of what I do and I have the freedom to put it into one of three classes: bill-paying, pocket money and pro bono. The two latter categories are only possible because I have the first one sorted. There are times I will do work for less than a living rate, or even for free (you're holding such an example in your hands now), but that is my choice, no one else's.

Quite simply, work out how much you need to earn per day, or even per hour, to cover all your fixed expenses and contribute to your household costs and live comfortably, and charge that. Charge at least that. The National Union of Journalists publishes recommended rates, worked out by professionals who have been where you are now. And they are minimal, so don't be afraid to go higher. Value your own work and show other people that you do. 'If you think a professional is expensive,' so the saying goes, 'try hiring an amateur.'

To sum up: giving up the day job isn't just something you do. It is something you must work towards. I was able to go full-time freelance because I had previously put in a couple of decades' worth of hard work and reputation-building. I was also flexible enough to take the work that came along. I started with a guarantee of a year's work and absolutely no promise of any more beyond that time. As it turns out, I have been able to keep going by adapting to a range of genres. In some ways I'm no different from any office-based worker on a fixed-term contract. In others, it's a bit like driving along a road after dark. All you can see in your headlights is the road ahead. You have no knowledge of where the road is going, or even a guarantee that it exists. In the day job, I learned to rely on God because I had nothing else. I like to think I still do.

Ben Jeapes was first published professionally in 1990 and has been a full-time ghostwriter since 2015. He thinks of himself as a writer whose work spans two millennia.

God's Plans, Not Mine

Nicki Copeland

First of all, I'd like to say how delighted we at Instant Apostle are to be publishing this book in partnership with ACW. And congratulations on reaching fifty years! A very significant milestone!

I've been a member of ACW for a few years now, and I have benefited greatly from the organisation in that time – from friends I have made to writers' days to other contacts and all sorts of really helpful information. And I hope in this article to bring some thoughts from all the different hats I wear – those of writer, editor and proofreader, and now publisher as well.

Shy book-lover

My own journey in the world of writing was, to be honest, a very unexpected one. I remember being at primary school and hiding my creative writing book in my desk when it was time to hand it in, as I just hadn't been able to put pencil to paper and think of anything to write in the lesson. This was something that continued for many years of my life – the feeling of not having anything worthwhile to say. I went on to study English at A level, which of course involved writing essays, but I know my lack of conviction in my own thoughts and opinions showed through in my efforts.

So I have to acknowledge the irony that God would set me on a path to become a writer. I guess it goes to show that, certainly for me, writing is a God-given gift. While I still struggle at times to believe I have anything to say that anyone else might find remotely interesting, I also acknowledge that writing is a way that God chooses to speak to me and through me. It's a way of processing my thoughts. I learn so much through the research process when writing an article, a chapter of a book, a talk, or a sermon. And I trust that God uses my words to speak to others too.

I've always loved books. As a child I was an avid reader. So when my first job was for a publishing house in London, I was very excited! However, a year and a half later the company moved away from London, and I was made redundant. I then worked in the African franchise division of Cadbury Schweppes for a number of years (on the soft drinks side, so no free chocolate for me, sadly), until I had my children.

Once they were at school and I had a bit more time on my hands, I undertook a distance-learning proofreading course, which brought me back into the publishing world as a freelance. This suited me well, as I could work from home within school hours and after the children were in bed. From there I moved into copy editing, working mainly on Christian books, which was such a joy. What a delight to be able to read for a living – it almost felt too good to be true!

Digging deep

Very unexpectedly, I found myself wanting to write my own words – not just to work on other people's. There was something inside me that needed to speak out. Believe me, no one was more surprised than I was! And I was even more surprised when the manuscript that I eventually wrote was accepted for publication by Instant Apostle (this was before I had much involvement with the company).

However, God's plan for my first book was rather different from mine. In my discussions with the publisher about the manuscript, he felt that it needed more personal stories, more about me and my own story. Then the old lack of confidence reared its head again. 'It's not supposed to be about me,' I countered. 'No one will want to read about me. I don't have anything interesting to share about myself.'

But he kept pushing – and I'm thankful he did, as he clearly was hearing God's voice. It was a really difficult process, and I had to dig deeper than I ever thought possible, but in the end, all the original stuff I'd written was stripped out, and what was left was the story of my journey through my struggles with low confidence and low self-esteem. More irony!

I've since had the unexpected privilege of speaking and sharing my story at conferences and other meetings, and I quickly realised how important it is that that we talk about our struggles and what God is doing in us. We can be sure that if we are struggling with an issue, there are other people wrestling with that same problem. If we are open about our challenges, rather than leaving us in a place of weakness, as we might think, it actually brings strength and encouragement, both to us and to others. When we bring things into the light, they lose their power over us.

Releasing others

As time went on, I continued my freelance editing and proofreading work. Although I work in other areas too, I really love working on Christian books – whether copy editing, proofreading or publishing them. I love the stories they tell. I love the wisdom they contain. I love the way they point to Jesus and His gospel. I love hearing the stories of how books change peoples' lives.

Over the years, I gradually became more involved with Instant Apostle – first copy editing and proofreading, then managing the editorial process, and then, in 2019, taking over the day-to-day running of the company. Another surprise!

There are many things I enjoy about my work with Instant Apostle, but one of them is working with new, previously unpublished writers. To receive a submission that clearly needs work, yet has something – to be able to see the potential in it, and to work with the rest of the team and the author through the whole process, until they (and I) eventually hold their book in their hands – it's such a privilege.

God gives messages to all sorts of people – not just to well-known speakers and writers – and it's a joy to release those messages and those writers and to watch where God takes them. It's also wonderful to hear the stories of how God is using the writers and the books to reach people, to encourage them, to challenge them, to help them wrestle with the difficult questions of life, and whatever else God might want to do. The day we received an email to let us know that someone had given their life to Jesus as a result of reading one of our books, there was much rejoicing here on earth, let alone in heaven (Luke 15:10)!

For me, writing, editing and publishing is truly a privilege. But it's also a responsibility. We have a duty before God to ensure that what we write and publish is theologically sound and is honouring to Him and His kingdom. But it's also a real joy, and I can't imagine myself working in any other industry.

Instant Apostle – to publish or not to publish?

Instant Apostle publishes a rather eclectic mix of genres – from memoir to mission and ministry, from fiction to devotional. So what, might you ask, is our criteria for accepting a manuscript?

Mainly, we need to believe that there is a message in it that God wants to be shared. It might be someone's own personal story that will encourage others. It might be teaching or ministry that offers a new perspective on age-old truths. It might be a fictional story that raises questions or deals with topical issues, or provokes readers to ask questions about the big issues of life.

We are a small publisher and we might not always sell huge quantities of a particular title. There is much emphasis on author promotion these days, from both large and small publishers, as well as what we can offer. But it isn't always about big numbers.

Didn't Jesus speak about leaving the ninety-nine to look for the one sheep (Matthew 18:12-14)? Sometimes a book might just be for a few, but if it makes a difference to those few, that's important.

I love reading fiction, so it's no surprise that I love to publish it too. Instant Apostle feels called to publish fiction that can cross over into the general market and appeal to non-Christians as well as to Christians. What we look for are what we call 'kingdom themes' – manuscripts that wrestle with topics but don't seek to give people the answers in neat, tidy boxes; life isn't like that. We're looking for manuscripts that will raise questions and encourage people to search for the answers for themselves, to discover the treasure of the kingdom of God.

Nicki Copeland is a freelance writer, speaker, copy editor and proofreader. She is the author of Losing the Fig Leaf *and* Less than Ordinary? *She is also responsible for the day-to-day running of Instant Apostle publishers. When she has the luxury of some free time, she can invariably be found with a book in one hand and some chocolate in the other. Find out more at www.nickicopeland.co.uk.*

A Little Bit of Independence

Wendy H Jones

When asked if I would be willing to write a 'tools of the trade' article for the ACW jubilee anthology, I was both delighted and honoured. The association has been a part of my journey since I wrote my first word, and the support and guidance of the members has been vital to my success. And I would consider my writing journey to be a success. There have been highs and there have been lows, but the journey has been exhilarating and I consider myself blessed. While this chapter is not my story, it is very deeply rooted in my story of being a multi-published, award-winning author making a living from my writing. I am known as a hybrid author where I am both independently and traditionally published, so I have a foot in both camps. Hence the reason for the title of this chapter – 'A Little Bit of Independence'.

Before doing so, I would like to talk a little bit about history. Did you know that authors such as Charles Dickens, Marcel Proust and Beatrix Potter were self-published? Then the pendulum swung the other way and self-publishing became synonymous with vanity publishing and was seen as something rather nasty. The only thing you can rely on in this world is that everything you are completely certain of will change. The pendulum is now swinging the other way once more with self- or independent publishing becoming increasingly popular. It is no longer seen as something to be ashamed of, but as a valid and highly professional route to publishing. The Society of

Authors advocates for self-publishing alongside more traditional methods. Many authors now choose to do this rather than go down the traditional publishing route, citing numerous reasons why they are doing so. Let me unpick these reasons and allow you to make an informed choice.

Overall control of decisions about your books and your business is one of the top reasons given for going the independent route. You decide every aspect of your book from title to cover design, from genre to distribution. Literally everything is under your control. Now, don't get me wrong, I am not saying you don't need help, and we will get to that further on in the discussion.

In addition to the above there are a number of spin-offs from controlling every aspect of the business. As I write, there is an ongoing discussion in the publishing world around eBook pricing. While this is not the place to go into the arguments for and against the pricing structure used by the big publishers, indie authors are free to set their own prices and therefore stand apart from that debate. Having the freedom to control your own pricing is a distinct advantage when it comes to being an indie author. I can set any price I want and change it whenever I want so, if I want to run a promotion or some paid advertising, I can lower my price accordingly. Appropriate pricing can give an advantage when it comes to readers buying books. Priced too high and readers think they are being ripped off. I appreciate that books are good value but often our brains tell us otherwise. Too low, and readers think the books can't be worth much – unless it's a promotion, of course, and they will buy that bargain in their droves.

The next spin-off is that you can release books as often as you want. Running a series and want to release one a month for twelve months? Go for it. Want to bring out one self-help book a month? Go for it. If readers like your book, they will be waiting for the next one. The quicker you get another book out, the higher the read-through rate. Please don't think I am advocating shoddy work. Nothing could be further from the truth. Speed should never take precedence over quality. But the premise that the more books you have out, the more you will sell, is true.

Now we've explored the *Why*, let's explore the *How* of independent publishing. While space and word count will not allow me to go into every detail, I will give you some top-notch advice to get you started.

My first piece of advice is professionalism. As I said previously, self-publishing should never be used as an excuse for pushing out shoddy work. Your books should be professional in every way, including editing, formatting and cover design. Hire a professional editor and professional cover designer – it will pay off in the end. Yes, it will cost you money, but no one said self-publishing was free. Even if you have a degree in English or your mate can pick up typos in books, still hire a professional editor and proofreader. We do not see the mistakes in our own work, as our brains will see what we think we wrote, not what is actually there. This does not mean send your first draft to an editor. Always edit and re-edit first. This will mean your draft is cleaner, it will take the editor less time and will not cost you as much money. Cut out extraneous passages and words so your word count is more realistic. Most editors charge per word and if you have 20,000 unnecessary words it's going to cost you a lot of money.

Professional cover design is equally as important. The saying is, 'You can't judge a book by its cover.' Sorry to burst your bubble, but everyone does. If they don't like the cover, they don't pick it up. Equally true is that an eye-catching cover may get someone to buy your book even if they don't read in your genre. I know, I've bought books in those circumstances.

Formatting your book professionally is also part of ensuring your book looks fantastic and follows the established industry not only in standards, but in expectations. Your book should be professional in every single way. I use a programme called vellum.pub to format my books. This does cost money and is only available for Apple Mac computers, but it is the best money

I have ever spent. If you haven't got a Mac, you can use Mac in the Cloud or pay someone with Vellum to format your book. It will be worth every penny. Vellum makes sure you have the correctly formatted book files for Kindle, Kobo, Nook, Apple Books, print and a generic ePub PDF file for any other use.

My next piece of advice is publish widely. This means making sure your book is available everywhere, not just shackling yourself to Amazon. I use Amazon for Amazon eBooks and Draft2Digital to distribute to every other eBook platform. This means my eBooks are available everywhere an eBook can be purchased. When it comes to paperbacks, use Amazon for those sold by Amazon and make sure you switch off expanded distribution. Then use Ingram Spark to distribute your books to bookshops and libraries. This means your books are available literally everywhere. If you look for any of my books in a bookshop anywhere in the world, you will see they are available. It's remarkable, mind-blowing and exciting, all in one.

I know this has not been a step-by-step guide to independent book publishing, but that is a whole book in itself. What I hope it has been is enough to show you that self-publishing is not only possible, but worth doing. I believe in self-publishing and am making a full-time living from my books. I have won an international award and spoken at conferences worldwide. Being independent does not mean that doors are closed to you; it means that you are able to push those doors and see where they lead.

Another option is to be both independently and traditionally published – a hybrid author. I have chosen to go down this route. My books for adults, both fiction and non-fiction, are published by me. My children's books are published by Malcolm Down and Sarah Grace Publishing. I don't know enough about publishing children's books, so it made sense for me to seek a publisher. I know my strengths and limitations, and this is what leads to success. I embrace every aspect of the publishing world.

In addition to writing and publishing books, I am also passionate about supporting others in their journey, to give back to others using all I have learned. To that end I have brought out a series of books under the banner 'Writing Matters'. So far there are two – *Motivation Matters* and *Marketing Matters* – but *Self-Publishing Matters* will be out by the time you are reading this book.

I will finish by saying my journey as an author has been wild, exhilarating and the greatest of my life. I would encourage you to explore indie publishing and not write it off. You never know where it might lead.

Wendy H Jones is an award-winning, international best-selling Scottish author who writes adult crime books, young adult mysteries, children's picture books and non-fiction books for writers. She is also a writing and marketing coach, runs the Writing Matters Online School *and is the* CEO *of* Authorpreneur Accelerator Academy *and the president of the Scottish Association of Writers, and hosts* The Writing and Marketing Show *podcast. She runs two writing groups: City Writers and History Writers. A committed Christian, she attends a New Frontiers church.*

Writing Competitions

Sophie Neville

> Write the vision
> And make *it* plain on tablets,
> That he may run who reads it.
> *Habakkuk 2:2 (NKJV)*

Thanks to ACW's Facebook page, I heard about a novel-writing contest organised by Athanatos Christian Ministries in the USA. Having made it to the shortlist, I was provided with a mentor to develop my first novel. They invited me to an awards ceremony and, to my amazement, I won 'The Grand Prize' of US$2,500, which came with an offer of publication. This was a huge encouragement. Another draft went on to win A Woman's Write and an Eyelands book award for an unpublished historical novel.

In 2020, I entered a second manuscript into the Association of Christian Writers' novel-writing competition judged by Tony Collins and Fay Sampson. I was honoured to be awarded third prize. The feedback was immensely useful and helped me to rewrite, keeping up the tension in my final chapters. On top of the prize, I was offered exposure in ACW's magazine *Christian Writer* and gained the confidence to submit the novel to major publishers.

Simply entering these competitions motivated me into honing my prose and working on blurbs, chapter breakdowns and synopses of different lengths, along with tailored author biographies. Speaking at an ACW writers' day, Amy Boucher Pye suggested that authors hire editorial help when making submissions of any kind. 'You only get one chance,' she emphasised. Composing a covering letter alone takes time, but it is essential that nothing is sent without being edited and proofread.

Some competition entry forms challenge the writer to think again. They put you through the refiner's fire, forcing you to consider how best to reach your audience. A new writing competition called Discoveries Women's Prize asked what had inspired me.

In composing and recomposing a synopsis, authors often find a crucial point or another twist that can be added to what was originally considered a finished story. Writing competitions also help you to take the step of selling your work, either by self-publishing or approaching an agent or publisher. They engender the endurance and persistence needed while presenting you with deadlines.

There are loads of competitions for poetry, short stories and flash fiction, as well as for full-length novels and screenplays, both unpublished and published. There are fewer for non-fiction, but I have been sharing those I hear about on the ACW Facebook page. Lists of writing awards can be found online with a chapter entitled 'Prizes and Awards' listed in the *Writers' & Artists' Yearbook*, which also lists grants, bursaries and fellowships. Some are regional, some are aimed at women, some are age related. Some are for crime novels, others for romance. Penguin Random House has been looking for Christmas love stories. There are a few for self-published books. Some are judged anonymously, some like to know all about the author. Sometimes the entry is free but most charge a fee. Bursaries or sponsored entries exist for some. ACFW – the Association of Christian Fiction Writers in the USA – offers two contests a year for unpublished novel writers, delivering detailed feedback from sincere Christian readers. The list of what they are looking for can prove a blessing in itself.

A few competitions, such as Book Pipeline or Roadmap, offer themselves as windows to Hollywood and provide readers' feedback. Some exist to help market editorial services; many are organised by literary agents or publishing houses, obviously charging a fee for talent-spotting. Agents and publishers themselves send manuscripts off for awards the whole time – or should do. The more well-known prizes for published books often demand huge entry fees. They are marketing platforms in themselves. Some seem to dish out awards to celebrities on condition they appear at the ceremony. Do research and chase this up yourself. My publisher failed to send in one of my non-fiction memoirs for a regional award that would have been enormously helpful in promoting the book.

Prizes can include cash, mentoring, agent introduction, writing retreats, inclusion in an anthology, publication in a magazine and even publishing deals. Some will be accompanied by awards ceremonies and substantial publicity.

There are so many competitions, I would suggest only entering those that are in line with your plans. Rejection is often mute. You may hear nothing more than confirmation of entry, but keep trying. A friend of mine working in finance cheerfully assured me, 'If you throw enough mud, some of it will stick.' I find the deadlines spur me on. Watch out for ensnaring traps. It is possible that some online 'awards' are fraudulent, others promise appalling 'book deals'. You don't want to sign your rights over!

Always read the rules very carefully before applying. They change every year. Don't enter too early, as you may redraft, but don't leave it until the last minute. You may encounter a technical problem with the site or need to contact the organisers. I realised I needed bulldog clips to enter a novel to the Irish Writers Centre and found myself running down the high street in flip flops, wondering where I could buy some before the post office closed.

Given the choice, I prefer to send in entries on paper, but most ask for submissions online. You certainly learn how to edit a header.

Many require a PayPal account. Prize money can come back via PayPal, which alarmed me somewhat. You do need to declare this on your HMRC tax return. I am advised it constitutes 'marketing' and it will, if you are successful. I know of London PR companies that employ personnel purely to apply for awards in the field of product promotion.

The demands of the entry forms alone can make you feel like pulling out chunks of hair, but the hard work involved makes winning all the more uplifting. It will undoubtedly raise you up and help sell the finished product. Book awards are loved by publishers and give readers confidence. They provide journalists and those organising literary festivals with a handle. You get to write 'award-winning author' in your biography, on your Amazon page and the cover of your books. It might even fire your creativity. Jackie Gooding's poem, 'My Writing Journey', published in *Christian Writer* reflects this:

> An essay I wrote at age ten,
> And won a prize-cup – then
> My poem was praised:
> My profile was raised
> I composed again and again.

I was once at a low point medically, lying in bed recovering from painful and intrusive biopsies, when a well-wrapped package arrived by post. It turned out to be a cut-glass trophy. I had won third prize in the International Rubery Book Awards for a self-published Christian testimony. Being no more than an illustrated diary designed as light reading, it was not worthy of first prize, but recognition for the hard work that went in to producing the book lifted my spirits enormously. I had totally forgotten that I'd entered the competition. The blessing was that this helped me win a place on one of the first Curtis Brown creative writing courses, since they were looking for prize-winning students. I was in a small class, which included Jane Harper, author of the bestselling crime novel *The Dry* (Little, Brown, 2016), now adapted into a film made on location in Australia.

I am truly grateful for the time put in by volunteers from the Association of Christian Writers who organise and judge competitions, featured in every issue of the magazine. Like readings and events, they are a real asset to an author and offer participation to isolated writers around the country. Why not enter a few literary competitions? It would be great even to be long listed.

After publishing a series of memoirs entitled The Making of Swallows and Amazons *(1974),* Funnily Enough *and* Ride the Wings of Morning, *Sophie Neville is developing historical novels set in Africa.*

Loneliness and the Christian Writer

Maureen Chapman

Writing is a lonely job. Writers need to be alone as they write, needing to focus on their subconscious, to allow ideas and words to flow through the brain and out on to paper or the screen of a computer. After the words are out in the open, then the real, unglamorous work begins: editing, finding mistakes and gaps, the patient rewriting, developing, polishing until the work is as good as it needs to be. At some point self-doubt creeps in. Loss of confidence, a block where an error is obvious. But how to deal with it? Where to turn for help?

In the early days of ACW, on one writers' day I listened to the speaker, Marion Stroud, then ACW chair. She stated from personal experience that writing as a Christian is costly, because we write the truth, and often truth is derided, attacked or disbelieved. Christian values are not popular in many places, and to be published can be difficult. Our writing comes from a different place, inspired by Bible truths and the Holy Spirit.

How, as Christian writers, do we deal with that kind of situation? Where do we find the empathic support, understanding and advice that we need?

The Association of Christian Writers came into existence to be a strong support system to help and inspire fellow Christian writers. We come from a wide spectrum of the Christian faith, which carries the potential for discord, criticism (which is often painful!) and arguments. We live in many locations, from cities, towns and villages in the UK to remote corners of the world. Some have chronic illnesses and are confined to their bedrooms. Some live busy and demanding lives, draining them of energy, while others have plenty of spare time and energy, the ability to think and meditate. Each one of us is unique, though, with a unique talent given to us by God.

From the beginning, a quiet emphasis has been laid on the need to accept other people's points of view, including their experience of God. Learning to show mutual respect and loving-kindness is an important part of developing our own writing skills and using them effectively. When we feel accepted and supported and share a mutual empathy with other people's experiences, our own work becomes enriched.

Having identified the needs of the Christian writer and now knowing what we were aiming for, a step-by-step action plan was put in place in order to meet them. This was a time of pre-electronic communications, of course, which meant we relied heavily on post, telephone conversations and face-to-face meetings.

Twice-yearly writers' days were organised successfully, mostly in London. Each one would begin with a short devotional section, followed by one or more speakers and workshops organised around a particular genre of the written word. There would also often be a question-and-answer session with the speaker, and individual five-minute slots to pitch work to an editor. These became lively sessions! Over coffee and lunch, we had opportunities to meet and chat with other writers. Some would become writing buddies and, in many cases, the friendships lasted for decades. I myself have three writing buddies dating back to the early 1990s.

But, out of the many hundreds who joined ACW in the beginning, only a few handfuls could attend these London and regional writers' days, limited by work, distance to travel and possible overnight stays, family commitments, finance or health. So local groups began to spring up, covering most of the

UK. For a few years there was even one in Cyprus. These remain vital today, people opening their homes or church halls to fellow local writers, organising their own meetings and speakers, even producing anthologies.

Understanding that even the local groups were hard to get to for some members, postal groups were started. These were the days before Jiffy bags, and individual work was posted in a green, cloth-covered large packet, affectionately known as the 'envelope'. Various genres were covered, and members enclosed typed copy of a story or article, poetry or even just rough ideas, to be commented on by the other members. Each member generally received the envelope about four times a year, or less frequently if it were scheduled to arrive during a holiday or sickness absence, and we had a week to respond and post it on. It was like Christmas, receiving a special present! We would carefully snip the stitching, taking the cloth off to open the envelope, and eagerly read each other's work and the various comments, not just on one's own writing but on everyone else's. Then came the painstaking task of restitching the package ready to post on.

ACW developed a postal critiquing service, which still exists today. A writer can send in a piece of work for advice, critique and general feedback on a one-to-one basis with an experienced writer, for a modest fee. The genres covered include poetry, writing for children, adult fiction, drama, non-fiction and short-story writing.

As a tool of connection and information, a postal newsletter/short magazine began, which morphed into *Candle & Keyboard*. Eventually, this grew into the present magazine *Christian Writer*, posted out to every paid-up member and including, among the articles, the details of area groups, competitions, committee members, etc.

Ever looking to extend its concern for fellow writers, ACW joined with Media Associates International and we learned something of the plight of Christian writers around the world bravely writing and publishing in their own hostile homelands and facing persecution. We began to raise funds to help them study and attend international conferences, and prayed for them.

Prayer partners were appointed to exercise a prayer ministry responding, in confidence, to specific requests by members needing help.

Fast forward to the internet age. In the last few years, there has been an explosion of new ways of communicating with each other online, including the ACW Facebook page, the ACW prayer group, the ACW More than Writers blog and the bi-monthly eNews bulletin – to say nothing of Twitter, Instagram and the rest.

Heart-warming also, since the arrival of COVID, is the chance to connect via Zoom. Local groups can now meet online and group leaders can share expertise and ideas, allowing ACW to keep moving forward. Those who are skilled in teaching are rising up to give lessons and host discussions online. New doors are opening, new undreamed-of opportunities are arising and we are being called to move into the future as the Holy Spirit guides us.

In recent years, the ACW prayer group has been well used and some wonderful answers to prayer have encouraged us all. COVID-19, with its on/off restrictions and on/off lockdowns, increased our loneliness and many of us felt we'd reached the end of the road. Exhausted and beset by difficulties, members have turned to ACW for help. It is heartening to read the various responses and support given to those brave enough to admit their needs. Especially encouraging are the writings and testimonies of those who suffer chronic illness, who live with constant pain and are only able to write for short periods of time. Their sweet words of grace, peace and even joy, shared as poetry, prayers or meditations, have challenged those of us who are able-bodied and have freedom to move and live outside the sick room. Whatever difficulties we may face – and each one of us has our own battleground – we are united by knowing that the ultimate place to find help is in God, whom we all worship and serve.

Remember Jesus' words from John 15:4: 'Remain in me, as I also remain in you. No branch can bear fruit by itself; it must remain in the vine. Neither can you bear fruit unless you remain in me.' We do not bear the burden of loneliness alone. God is with us in all our creativity and will never leave us. We need to make sure we are connected to the vine, receiving the nourishment and inspiration we need. Whatever the future holds for us as lonely writers, ACW is poised to continue to grow and evolve in new ways, equipping us and supporting us to serve God with the talents He has given us. Together we will be fruitful, and our words will be like a light in a dark world.

Maureen Chapman is a retired missionary nurse/midwife, hotelier, minimarket owner and now writer and gardener. She started ACW's postal writing groups.

Taking Care of Ourselves: Health and Safety for Writers

Jane Walters

The idea of safeguarding our health and well-being at work might have dominated society's thinking in recent years, but it's hardly a new one. The first health and safety legislation introduced in this country dates back to 1802 with the Health and Morals of Apprentices Act. In 1974, the Health and Safety at Work Act (followed by the Management of Health and Safety at Work Regulations 1999) drew attention like never before to the need for safe working practices for all employees in the workplace. For the freelance or creative writer, thoughts of 'safe working practices' might be eclipsed by our more creative endeavours, but there are a number of important issues that need to be addressed in order to protect our health and well-being, whether that be physical, mental/emotional or spiritual.

Physical

The physical aspects of writing concern the correlation between the place we do it and the bodies we use.

Whatever the working environment – a kitchen, bedroom or specially purposed office – there should be adequate *ventilation*. This not only helps regulate the temperature but also reduces humidity and circulates fresh air, expelling airborne pollutants and carbon dioxide. Research conducted by Reading University showed a direct association between environmental conditions and pupils' cognitive performance in the classroom, with an unwelcome build-up of CO_2 proving a significant factor.[13]

There is no specific UK legislation regarding *working temperatures*, but it's generally accepted that the optimum range is between 16°C and 24°C.[14] Lower temperatures lead to a loss of concentration and increased tiredness, while higher temperatures can also lead to reduced concentration and slippery hands – pretty hopeless for holding a pen or controlling a keyboard!

As long ago as the nineteenth century, a condition known as scrivener's palsy (writer's cramp) was identified among writers.[15] Coming from overuse of the writing hand, it's one of several painful *repetitive strain injuries* that writers can fall victim to, which sometimes require surgery. While simply taking a break to let the muscles rest goes without saying, the impact of the *ergonomics* of the writing space can't be ignored.

The Mayo Foundation recommends the following set-up for computer use:[16]

- The monitor should be an arm's length away from the face, with the top of the screen at eye level.
- Wrists should be held straight or slightly raised when typing, with hands at or below elbow level. Avoid dorsiflexion, where the fingers reach upwards to touch the keys.
- Supporting the weight of the arms will reduce pain in the neck and shoulder muscles. If there are armrests, they should be positioned so that the shoulders stay relaxed.

13 www.reading.ac.uk/news-archive/press-releases/pr18842.html (accessed 8th January 2021).
14 www.gov.uk/workplace-temperatures (accessed 8th January 2021).
15 www.jnnp.bmj.com/content/76/4/513 (accessed 27th January 2021).
16 www.mayoclinic.org/healthy-lifestyle/adult-health/in-depth/office-ergonomics/art-20046169 (accessed 8th January 2021).

- The chair height should be adjusted so that knees are about level with the hips.
- Use a chair that supports the shape of the spine and make sure its height allows your feet to be flat on the floor. Use a footrest if necessary.

Even with the desk area set up correctly, we need to be aware that our bodies weren't designed to sit for too long but work better when they can bend and flex. It's common knowledge that a sedentary lifestyle can increase the risk of a range of chronic diseases, including obesity, type 2 diabetes and high blood pressure.[17] Consider joining the ranks of our illustrious literary forebears who stood to do their writing. Hemingway, Nietzsche, Dickens, Nabokov, Lewis Carroll, Virginia Woolf and many others used a standing desk. Standing can also serve to remind us to walk around at regular intervals, adding in some stretches if necessary, so that our bodies do not suffer for our art.

Being *well hydrated* not only keeps our bodies comfortable but can also boost productivity by up to 14 per cent.[18] In men, reduced hydration leads to increased fatigue and anxiety, while in women it can cause decreased concentration, depression and headaches. It is therefore recommended that we have access to water whenever we are writing.

Eye-care is important. When we work at a computer, or are concentrating hard on the page, we tend to blink less often, which can lead to dry eyes. Make a conscious effort to blink more and use hydrating eye drops if eyes become sore. Looking away from the monitor towards an object in the distance can help relieve eye strain. Try the 20:20:20 rule: every twenty minutes, look at something that's twenty feet away for around

---

[17] www.medicalnewstoday.com/articles/322910 (accessed 25th March 2021).
[18] www.uel.ac.uk/research/health-promotion-and-behaviour/hydration-nutrition-and-cognition (accessed 26th January 2021).

twenty seconds.[19] It's worth adjusting monitor screen settings so that the light level is comfortable.

With writers spending so much time indoors, there is a risk of *vitamin D deficiency*. I myself was diagnosed as deficient through a routine blood test, unaware I had most of its symptoms, which include:

- Muscular weakness;
- Heavy sensations in the legs;
- Chronic musculoskeletal pain;
- Fatigue or easy tiring;
- Frequent infections;
- Depression.

Vitamin D deficiency can only be diagnosed through a blood test and, following extensive reading on the subject, I would urge every writer to ask their GP for a test. Vitamin D is produced by the sun's rays on the skin and should be a natural process. However, most of us spend too long inside and, when we do venture out, we use sunscreen, which inhibits the production of vitamin D. It is the suggestion of experts such as Soram Khalsa, MD, that we should all be taking a daily supplement.[20] It is extremely difficult to take too much of the vitamin and highly likely that, without help, our levels are naturally too low and thereby cause us physical and mental difficulty.

Mental health and welfare

Having considered the importance of physical well-being for the writer, our attention must turn to the equally vital issue of mental good health. If I break my leg or my back aches, I can

---

[19] www.healthline.com/health/eye-health/20-20-20-rule#symptoms (accessed 8th January 2021).

[20] Soram Khalsa, *The Vitamin D Revolution* (London: Hay House, 2009).

still write; but if my mind is suffering then it's a different story (no pun intended!).

For the creative writer, there are considerable *mental and emotional benefits*.[21] Being creative:

- Relieves stress. Creative activities have the same effect on our systems as engaging in meditation.
- Renews brain function. Making art involves both hemispheres of the brain, helping to improve and restore communication between different parts of the brain. Memory function can also be enhanced.
- Improves mood, partly through the distraction of creating and partly through self-awareness and catharsis.
- Can boost the immune system and help relieve pain.
- Offers fun and freedom of expression.

Though the benefits are many, there are some aspects to writing that can cause problems, and one is *social isolation*, since writing is often a solitary occupation.[22] It may be helpful to understand the distinction between solitude and isolation. Solitude can exist as a bubble within the company of other people – for example, when writing in a café or library – and it generally supports the creative process. Isolation, on the other hand, has more negative connotations and tends to hinder the creative process.

Whether being alone for long periods will cause problems or not may depend on whether we are extroverts or introverts. The measure of this is whether we get energised chiefly by our alone time or by the company of other people. The extrovert will struggle more in extended periods of being alone, and it is vital

---

[21] www.livealittlelonger.com/6-health-benefits-of-being-creative/ (accessed 19th January 2021); www.positivelypresent.com/2018/08/creativity.html (accessed 19th January 2021).

[22] www.becomeawritertoday.com/is-writing-lonely/ (accessed 19th January 2021).

for them in particular to break the feelings of isolation by meeting with others.

All of us, however, need the company of other people in our downtime, and part of our mental and emotional well-being is rooted in *connecting with others*. Laughing and sharing over a simple cuppa can be utterly restorative. Furthermore, I cannot overemphasise the importance of belonging to a writing association and especially a writers' group. Joining the Association of Christian Writers at the very outset proved pivotal to my own development as a writer. Nailing my colours to the mast, so to speak, was making a declaration to myself and others about the seriousness of my intent. More importantly, I made friends and allies with people who have been a constant encouragement. Sometimes, our sense of isolation comes not just from physical aloneness, but from our efforts being misunderstood by friends and family. Having fellow writers to connect with ensures that we have people who know only too well what we go through!

On the other hand, there may be some who crave aloneness. The demands of family life are not naturally conducive to finding time and space to write, and it's hard when the people we live with don't respect our need for quiet and lack of interruption. Part of our mental good health as writers is to be at peace as we work, and we may have to put boundaries around this part of our life so that it can flourish instead of being trampled.

I would recommend *walking* as part of the writer's toolkit. A little wander around the garden or any outdoor space offers not only fresh air and physical exercise, but a chance to clear the head.[23] If reasonable to do so, go for a daily walk. It is my own experience that letting my mind wander as I walk, getting distracted by my surroundings, can often release new ideas (which I jot into my notebook in case I forget by the time I get

---

[23] www.theguardian.com/lifeandstyle/2015/mar/25/a-good-walk-the-perfect-way-to-clear-your-head (accessed 25th March 2021).

home); but research confirms I'm not alone. In a study conducted by Oppezzo and Schwartz, they compared four groups of people trying to think of new ideas while either walking or sitting.[24] They found that walking, and especially walking outdoors, was the most effective, concluding, 'Walking opens up the free flow of ideas, and it is a simple and robust solution to the goals of increasing creativity and increasing physical activity.' Tom Cox, writing in *The Guardian*, goes further, claiming, not entirely tongue-in-cheek, that 'it's an official fact of writing that all books would be at least twice as good if they could be written while walking'.[25]

Spiritual well-being

As Christian writers, there is a further dimension to our self-care, and that is to attend to our spiritual needs. It doesn't matter whether we write overtly Christian material or not, the fact remains that our giftings are rooted in God and we hope that they will bring Him glory. The apostle Paul says it well: 'Whatever you do, work at it with all your heart, as working for the Lord, not for human masters, since you know that you will receive an inheritance from the Lord as a reward. It is the Lord Christ you are serving' (Colossians 3:23-24). When prayer underpins our efforts, the stress is lifted and joy invades our endeavours. Reading the Bible and other texts restores our perspective. We might be writing solo, but God is the source of wisdom, inspiration and motivation. I tend to light a candle as I'm writing, with a prayer that God would be present with me and that He would illuminate my mind, help me to see clearly and keep me focused. Meeting with our Christian community – whether that's church members or groups of writers – to enjoy

---

[24] M Oppezzo and D L Schwartz, 'Give Your Ideas Some Legs: The Positive Effect of Walking on Creative Thinking', *Journal of Experimental Psychology: Learning, Memory, and Cognition*, 40(4), 2014, pp1142-1152.
[25] www.theguardian.com/lifeandstyle/2015/mar/25/a-good-walk-the-perfect-way-to-clear-your-head.

their company and take advantage of their support is a vital part of our self-care too.

In conclusion, as writers, we have a duty of care to our bodies and minds – the very tools of our trade. Our aim is to achieve balance in our writing lives between:

- Comfort and efficiency;
- Fruitfulness and family and friends;
- Times of concentration and relaxation.

Write well!

Jane Walters is the author of Too Soon: a Mother's Journey through Miscarriage *(Jane Clamp, SPCK, 2018) and writes regularly for radio. Her novels are represented by Intersaga Literary Agency. She is vice-chair of ACW. www.janewyattwalters.com*

Defeating Our Writing Enemies

Janet Wilson

Writing enemies are varied, resourceful and sneaky! In this chapter we're going to have a look at a few, and consider some ways to defeat them. Let's start with a nasty one:

Self-doubt

The most common thing new writers ask me is, 'How do I know if my writing is good enough?'

Let me tell you, in my firmest voice, there's no such thing as 'good enough'.

Let me explain.

I'm assuming, if you're reading this, that you feel called to write. Suppose, instead of worrying about your ability, you decided to write, in the first place, for just one person who loves you. Someone who won't judge you. Does that relieve the pressure a bit?

We all have to start somewhere. When I first started knitting dolls for refugees, I was a bit shaky with the pattern, but now I've got better. Those first few dolls were less than perfect in different ways, but *they were good enough*. Not anything like good enough to sell in Harrods, but good enough for a child to love.

How special do you think your young relative/friend's child would feel if you were to write a story just for them? It might not be good enough for a publisher to take on, but it could blow the child's socks off, especially if it featured them and their pets, and they all went on adventures together! And suppose there's a message in that story that helps the child understand they have a Father in heaven who cares for them?

Or if you feel led to write devotionals, why not write a piece for a neighbour going through a tough time?

What if your story, poem or prayer only touches one, precious life? Wouldn't it all be worth it?

So what if it's not perfect? With practice and a willingness to learn, you can improve!

Maybe you can write your next story for a child known to you. Perhaps you might enter an article into a competition, publish a story on Kindle, self-publish a book, or even get a publishing contract...

But let's hold all that lightly. Let's start with one piece of writing, for one person – or the next person.

You can do it. Your writing is good enough. It's time to get to work.

Still not sure? Perhaps you are suffering from imposter syndrome!

Imposter syndrome

Imposter syndrome is a real thing, and it can be an ugly giant standing between us and our writing.

Here's the biggest clue that you are suffering from imposter syndrome: you live with the fear that someone's going to find out that you really shouldn't be a writer at all! You feel unworthy, insecure, a fraud.

But if we allow ourselves to be defeated by imposter syndrome, our books/articles/poems/prayers won't get written.

Who then misses out? Your readers. My readers. All of our readers.

But how do you know you're *not* an imposter?

Good question! Here's the test: *If you want to write/feel led to write, give it a go.*

And that's it.

I still struggle with imposter syndrome sometimes. Aren't there people so much more accomplished than me who could write, teach and publish? Of course! But I have come to realise:

- There will always be people who write better stories than me.
- There will always be people who can teach better than me.
- There will always be people with more experience than me in publishing.

But the Lord has chosen to use *me*! So I need to get on with what I'm called to do, to the best of my ability.

Believe me, if God can use me, He can use you. There aren't any 'super people' about, so He has to use us!

To help you move forward, here are seven weapons you can use against your imposter syndrome giant:

- Be at peace with your current ability. You may not be brilliant right now, but that's OK, as long as you are willing to learn. We all have to hone our skills!
- Set a small goal. This can be as simple as deciding on names for your characters. Do that one step straight away! Then set a new step every day. Imposter syndrome will have to move out of the way as you see yourself getting your writing done.
- Write out your mission statement. Who are you writing for? Why? Why not print out a picture of who you are writing for and stick it over your computer, to remind you of your purpose?
- Stop worrying about what others think/comparing yourself with others. There will be people who mock, even kindly. Looking round at what everyone else is doing and saying isn't helpful. No one can write like you. God made you unique! Be unashamedly you, whatever you think

people are saying about you (they might not be saying anything, of course!).

- Persevere. We may never be able to completely banish all thoughts of what we conceive to be our inability, but we shouldn't let that stop us from moving forward.
- Surround yourself with other encouraging people/writers. Joining the ACW or a writers' group would be a good start. Getting a prayer partner or two is helpful.
- Stay close to God. Even when we are weak, we are strong (2 Corinthians 12:10), if we have God's Spirit living within us. Pray about your writing. Let God's Word be a 'lamp for [your] feet, [and] a light on [your] path' (Psalm 119:105). Let His words and His presence lead and guide you.

Ready to go? No? What if you are just feeling lazy? This is an enemy we all have to fight at times!

Laziness

This is what you need to do when you're slobbing on the settee with the TV remote, thinking about writing…

- Promise yourself you will write for just twenty minutes. After the twenty minutes you can go back to doing whatever, if you want to.
- Get up, without stopping to argue with yourself, and walk straight over to the computer.
- Switch the computer on and start straight away, remembering you promised yourself you can stop after twenty minutes.
- Do as much as you can in those twenty minutes (pretend your life depends on it).
- Keep going if you want to, or stop if you don't.

Then you do the same every day. Just twenty minutes.

This is what will happen:

- You will start to enjoy your twenty minutes.
- You may go on longer sometimes.
- Your novel (or other work) will start to take shape.
- Your laziness will drop away as you begin to see the end in sight.

Hope that helps – this is something that has worked for me. The big keys are to not give yourself time to argue with your lazy side, and keep the momentum going.

But what about distractions?

Distractions

We live in an age of distraction. Social media can take over our lives if we let it. Each time our phone pings we receive a rush of endorphins, and want (need?) to check it immediately. Will it be a message from a friend, or another email from an airline with amazing holiday deals?

And there are endless other distractions – the Amazon parcel arriving, dinner to prepare, the lady down the road who's ill… and that's not counting work, housework, the garden and all the paperwork that fills life…

Eek!

How does anyone ever get any writing done, ever?

Here are a few tips if you are often distracted:

- **Make writing part of your daily (or at least weekly) routine.** This is the biggest and best tip I can give you. If you always write on Tuesday evenings, or during your lunch break at work, it will become a habit and you won't have to think about it – you'll just do it. Everyone around you will expect you to do it too, which will help!

- **Make it easy for yourself.** Turn off your wi-fi. Leave your phone in another room. Put a 'Do Not Disturb' notice on the door and put the cute kittens in another room. Do it fast, so your brain doesn't get a chance to argue. (Aw, those kittens! I know, but they will still be there when you finish writing!)

- **Talk to yourself as if you were your best friend** (the encouraging one!). 'You know you can do this. What you are doing is important. You don't have to check on your aunt right now, do you?'

- **Get excited.** Tell your brain that your writing time is a privilege, a responsibility and also the most wonderful joy. It's going to be good! So when washing the kitchen floor seems more appealing, remember how much you love writing!

- **Accept that life happens.** Sometimes nothing will work. Hey ho! Smile and get back to plan as soon as you can. You're only defeated when you give up. And you're not going to do that, are you?

Janet Wilson is an author, speaker, founder of award-winning publishing house Dernier Publishing (Christian Fiction for Kids and Teens: www.dernierpublishing.com) and setter-upper of Write for a Reason (www.write-for-a-reason.com) – a resource for aspiring writers.

Submitting Your Manuscript

Fay Sampson

I have had two careers: teaching and writing. I love doing both. I enjoy critiquing manuscripts because it calls upon both skills. And it's a good feeling if I can help someone else move closer to publication.

Submitting a manuscript calls for the writer to put forward the best work they are capable of. Imagine a busy agent or editor receiving thousands of submissions a year. It isn't humanly possible to read all of them. These people become expert in casting their eye over the first few pages and consigning most of them to the reject pile. You need to do everything you can to keep your own manuscript in play.

I'm saddened by the number of authors who evidently haven't proofread their manuscripts before submitting them to me. If you want to become a professional writer, you need to work to a professional standard. It's one thing to make mistakes in punctuation, say, because you don't know a rule; it's quite another to get it wrong because you just haven't bothered to check. An editor will mark you down as slipshod and unreliable.

First impressions matter. Start with a good title page. This should contain four pieces of information: title of the work, author, author's full contact details, word count (to the nearest 1,000). If the book is part of a series, say so. Give the series title and the number of this volume.

You have automatic copyright in everything you write, even a shopping list. Publishers know this, so you don't need to include the © symbol.

Resist the temptation to embellish your title page artistically. Design is a matter for the publisher; yours is to provide the text.

Because the agent or editor may not look much beyond the first page, this needs to be good. Imagine a customer in a bookshop attracted by the cover and skimming the first page to decide whether to buy it. The opening has to be strong enough to make them turn over. In most cases, this will be the promise of a compelling plot, but it could be the sheer quality of the writing.

But before you even write that first page, you need to make an important decision. You have the gist of a novel in your head. Now ask yourself: whose story is this?

This decision will shape everything that follows. Is this one character's story, which can be told in the first person, or as a vividly imagined third-person narrative? Does it swing between two characters, both given more or less equal weighting? Do you want to widen the perspective by using a number of different viewpoints? Any of these strategies can work. What you must do is plan your narrative standpoint before you begin. If you simply plunge into the novel and grab at random viewpoint characters as you go along, the result will be a mess.

Never switch viewpoints within a scene. Ask yourself: whose scene is this? If your chief protagonist is present, it will almost always be their viewpoint that you need.

So, you have the outline of your story and the viewpoint character or characters. You've thought of a strong opening to hook your readers. What then?

Children often write stories that seem quite promising to begin with. But then they become a series of incidents which don't seem to be leading anywhere... and then... and then... and then...

What such stories lack is a key question to drive the plot. Something the reader will really care about and that will keep them turning the pages to find the answer. Classic key questions are: will she marry him? Whodunit? Can they save the planet from disaster?

There may be subplots, but never let this key question slip out of sight. The reader should be kept in suspense, wondering about the answer until just before the end.

And the end should not come too easily. There need to be high points of hope and low ones when the protagonist's aims are thwarted. A graph of the plot should be like the outline of a mountain range, with the peaks growing ever higher as you approach the climax. Play on the reader's emotions, as you swing them from highs to lows. And bring it to a satisfying conclusion – which need not be success in a more nuanced novel – just before the end, with a short final chapter to wind things up.

The strength of the plot will depend on what kind of novel you are writing. It obviously needs to be dramatic for crime fiction. It can be gentler in, say, a book about a couple's attempts to make a go of a smallholding. But the drama, the hopes, the highs and lows will still be there.

There are some exceptions, where plot matters very little. Few people really care about the plot in a P G Wodehouse novel. It is the joy of the comic writing that keeps readers hooked. Similarly, in a literary novel, it can be the sheer beauty of the writing, and the sensations it evokes, that keeps readers immersed. That said, many literary novels do have fine plots.

What should bring your plot to life now are the characters. Do you have a clear and vivid sense of them? If not, it may be helpful to sit down and write a page about each of them – appearance, background, family, work, hobbies, likes and dislikes, idiosyncrasies, relationships to other characters, etc. What makes that character uniquely interesting?

Your character's background and personality will affect the way they talk. Ideally, the reader should be able to tell who is speaking without your telling them, just through their distinctive voice. Think of each scene as a play, with the dialogue as your script. Imagine your characters speaking it.

I once wrote a novel in the voice of a pagan Dark Age blacksmith. He was so different from me that I spent two days in front of my computer, trying to hear whether I had got his voice right. When it came back from the publisher, a copy editor had changed the whole thing to the style of an Oxbridge essay! It should be your character speaking, not you.

The same attention to detail goes for your setting. As the author, you should know far more about this than you include in the book. Again, it may help to write at length about the settings you use. Bring them vividly to life and keep those pictures in your mind. When you come to write the novel, you won't use all of it. A single, telling detail will often say more than an attempt to paint the whole picture, and will linger longer in the mind.

So far, so good. You have your plot, characters and settings vividly imagined. All should be well, right?

But the biggest leap of imagination an author has to make is not to imagine the story, but to imagine yourself inside the reader's head. Your own is now teeming with colourful images, but the reader's is a blank canvas. The only images that appear on it will be the ones you paint there. Are the words you have put on the page really going to do the job? Will your readers now see what you see, or just a pale shadow of it? You may find it helpful to enlist a 'critical friend': someone who can be that blank-canvas reader and tell you honestly whether your words are achieving what you intended them to.

So much for the big questions, but your manuscript can let you down in other ways.

Punctuation is an essential tool of the writer. It's not just a question of pedantic rules. It tells the reader how you want the words to be read – rather like musical notation. Read your work aloud. If you make a slight pause, you probably need a comma there. A more positive break calls for a full stop.

There are some simple rules for dialogue that are often overlooked. You need to use a comma to separate the name of the person addressed from the rest of the speech. 'What is your dragon doing, Fritz?' Even writers who know this rule frequently forget it.

If you are shaky on punctuation, try this exercise. Copy out a page of a novel, omitting all punctuation marks, capital letters and paragraph breaks. Now close the book and try to reconstruct that page. Compare the two versions meticulously, down to the last comma. Mark any discrepancies in red and try to understand why you went wrong. Next day, repeat the exercise with a different page. Continue until good punctuation becomes instinctive.

Remember, you are submitting your manuscript in a hugely competitive field. Only the best will succeed. Make sure that your submission is as good as you can possibly make it.

Good luck.

Fay Sampson is the author of fifty-five books and editor for a writing consultancy. She is the ACW fiction adviser.

Better Late Than Never

Marion Field

I am sure I was born with a pen in my hand! As a child, I was always scribbling stories in a collection of exercise books. I was also a voracious reader. Growing up in a very strict Brethren group, we had no radio. Television was still in its infancy. Our house was full of books and my father and I spent many happy hours browsing in the local library. He introduced me to the classics and I was determined to read all Charles Dickens' books before I was twenty. I almost made it!

I continued to write, although my time was limited while I was at college training to teach; once qualified, I taught in England for several years before succumbing to my urge to travel. By now, I had left the Brethren. Having sampled several nonconformist chapels, I had finally joined my parents in the local Anglican church.

As I had relatives in Canada, I applied for a teaching post in Hamilton, Ontario, and decided to 'emigrate'. An exchange with a Canadian teacher was not an option as I would have received only my English salary, and the cost of living in Canada was considerably higher than in England. I had intended to stay only one year but it was four years before I finally returned home.

While in Hamilton, I continued to write and eventually I had my first success. I had written an account of watching a Canadian football match – very different from the English game! My father, who acted as my agent, submitted my article to the *Times Educational Supplement* and, to my delight, it was published. Sadly, I never reached such heights again!

My wanderlust was still rampant and after a few weeks in England, I set off for Uganda. For two years I taught English, physical education and music in an African girls' boarding school. It was a wonderful experience and provided plenty of material for articles. To my delight, several were published in the magazine *African World.*

Home again, I acquired a teaching post in a local school while I continued to write. I had never met any other writers, so I was very pleased when a friend offered to take me to a meeting of the Fellowship of Christian Writers. I found the group very welcoming, and I was intrigued by the talk given by one of the members, Christine Wood. She had just published her book, *Exclusive Bypath.* As I listened, I realised that she was talking about the same Exclusive Brethren group in which I had grown up! Her experience was different from mine so surely I, too, could write about my early life.

On the way home on the train, I scribbled down as much as I could remember about my upbringing. For the next few weeks, all my spare time was occupied with writing my autobiography. My parents and several friends helped by remembering events I had forgotten. At last, I completed the work to my satisfaction, checked it carefully and submitted it to several publishers. Eventually, they all rejected it. However, two of the editors were complimentary about my work. In the 1990s, self-publishing was becoming popular. Having just retired from teaching, I contemplated following that route. However, I needed confirmation. When I attended another meeting of the Fellowship of Christian Writers, I met Freda Harris and told her that I was thinking about self-publishing my work.

'Definitely go for it,' she assured me. 'My self-published book, called *The Fear Barrier,* is on the book table. You'll be very interested in one chapter. It's all about leaving the Exclusive Brethren; I left, like you, when they lost their biblical roots.'

'I asked the Lord for a sign,' I said excitedly. 'I think you have just given it to me.'

My autobiography, *Don't Call Me Sister!*, was self-published the following year. Not only did I sell all the published copies, but I won the David Thomas Award for the best non-fiction book self-published in 1994. Consequently, Highland Books, which had originally rejected my work, accepted my next proposal – a ghostwritten biography of another 'escapee' from the Brethren. My self-published autobiography was then republished by Highland Books.

I continued to attend the Christian writers' meetings. By now, it had changed its name to the Association of Christian Writers and, for several years, I acted as secretary for the group. Meanwhile, Freda had introduced me to How-to Books who were asking for writers. As an ex-head of an English department, I decided that I could use the material I had accumulated over my years of teaching. How-to Books accepted my first proposal and I wrote five more books for them. My best seller was *Improve Your Written English*. I was thrilled when one reviewer said of this book, 'If you never buy another reference book, buy this one.'

With Freda's sponsorship, I became a member of the Society of Women Writers and Journalists. Sylvia, one of the members, introduced me to Amberley Publishing who were looking for writers of local history. History had always fascinated me and I was delighted to write a history of my home town, Woking, for them. This publisher than commissioned me to write several more local history books. My twenty-sixth published book, *Woking A–Z*, came out at the beginning of 2020. I had planned to hold a launch in a local Greek restaurant which was mentioned in the book. However, like so many other things, that was put on hold because of the COVID-19 lockdown.

I have not wasted my time this year as I am currently working on a sequel to my autobiography. Over the years I have also written a number of poems. These have now been published using Amazon's Self-Publishing package. My account of my experiences teaching in England, Canada and Uganda is also waiting to be published in the same way.

I am very grateful to the members of the Association of Christian Writers for their help and support over the years. Freda Harris and Christine Wood are now with the Lord, but they were both instrumental in helping me to start on my writing journey. It was many years before I eventually became a published author so I hope my experience may encourage others also to persevere.

Marion Field is the author of twenty-six books and is the ACW non-fiction adviser. As mentioned above, she is currently working on a sequel to her award-winning autobiography.

Writing Devotional Articles

Amy Boucher Pye

When I opened the letter, I noticed that it came from a prison. The woman writing recounted how she had been crying out to God in fear, doubt and frustration: 'Why God? I can't. Really? Maybe I'm not yours. Where are you? I need you. Are you listening?' In the midst of her turmoil, her friend gave her a devotional and told her to read it. She felt too tired, but when she did, she wept.

She had read my article in *Our Daily Bread*, in which I shared how I had attended a church service with my parents. According to the usual practice, we held hands while saying the Lord's Prayer together: 'As I stood with one hand clasped to my mother's and the other to my father's, I was struck by the thought that I will always be their daughter. Although I am firmly in my middle age, I can still be called "the child of Leo and Phyllis". I reflected that not only am I their daughter, but I will also always be a child of God.'

Why did those words hit her so hard? She knew that 'God had this personally hand-delivered to assure me that I am His and He hears me' because her father is named Leo and her mother Phyllis! As she said, 'What are the odds?!'

I'm guessing the odds are pretty low. But the unseen agent at work is God, our loving parent who has all the resources of the world at His disposal. Letters such as this one remind me how He uses our offerings to bless others. God lovingly takes the seeds we sow as He plants, waters and tends them.

So how do we go about writing these short thoughts to inspire and encourage others in their journey with God? Here are some tips, born out of more than a decade of writing more than a thousand Bible-reading notes and devotionals.

Choose one big idea

I have to remind myself of this nearly every time I sit down to write an *Our Daily Bread* article; I so easily meander off the main path as I explore side trails. And every time I do, I make more work for my editor, for those bits will be cut.

Keeping to one idea means that you're making it easier for the reader to grasp that one thought. You might get frustrated because you have so many more connections you could make. I feel it too. Put those in a file for your next book or article, where you will have more room to explore them.

Gather your thoughts

In the days or weeks before your deadline, read through the text you've been assigned or that you've chosen, asking God to help you as you write. Keep a file on your device where you can jot down notes and illustrations.

As you know, as writers, we train ourselves to notice details – it's as if while we nearly hit the car in front of us we also note what we experience when that car stops suddenly. We take in the hue of the sky and how the light hits our eyes, the pounding feeling in our chest when our foot reflexively hits the brake and the car stops just in time, along with the prayer of, 'Thank You, Lord,' that we exhale.

Submit yourself to the text

Often I write Bible-reading notes that are assigned to me, such as two weeks on Hosea or a fortnight looking at Psalm 18 verse by verse. We often skip over the hard bits in the Bible, so writing on a larger portion of the text can help us to avoid this tendency. But by 'submit' I also mean that we seek to read not what we want to read in the Bible, but what God has put there. Do some research and find out the context. Don't just jump to handy conclusions. Ask God's Holy Spirit to reveal the meaning. Leading to...

Research

When I first started writing Bible-reading notes, I spent a week or more reading and taking notes on various Bible commentaries on the passage. I hadn't engaged with the Bible at that level before, and needed the help of those steeped in biblical studies. But in doing so much background reading, I was in danger of merely parroting back the ideas in the commentaries as I struggled to form my own opinion about the text. I had to put my notes aside for several days so that I could develop what I wanted to say about the passage.

I might not spend a whole week researching now, but I always make sure I consult several commentaries to delve more deeply into the original context and meaning. I also attribute my sources.

Journey with the reader

This probably doesn't need stating, but as a writer you're a fellow pilgrim and you'll often share what you're learning while you're writing. Wearing the clothes of humility makes our writing all the more welcoming and winsome to the reader.

Employ the classic formula

Devotionals often start with an arresting anecdote, which links to the biblical text, which leads to the application. This is the classic formula: illustration, text, application.

What are you writing – a one-off devotional? Then resorting to the familiar recipe is best. Are you penning part of a series? Then you have more latitude in breaking the rules of the formula. You might, for instance, have space to go deeper and to explore more. As the reader has committed to your series, you could start the day's reading by digging straight into the text and not including an anecdote to catch their attention.

Make your words (or characters) count

'If I had more time, I'd make this shorter.' Usually the text in a devotional article is limited to around three hundred words (or fewer), so the content really matters. One publisher I write for counts characters instead of words, so there's no fudging. Write your first draft and then prune and cut. Employ strong verbs – the passive voice eats up your word count. Delete adjectives and adverbs. And so on.

Pray

This is the most important element of writing devotionals. Pray before you start; pray while you're writing; pray while you're rewriting; pray when you send off your work to your editor. We trust that God will inspire us with His Word and we yearn for Him to bring just the right encouragement for the broken-hearted, the lonely, the overwhelmed. We often write a year in advance, so we can't control the outcome. That makes the sometimes miraculous encounters between devotionals and the reader's experience so humbling.

I can't explain how sometimes an illustration will pop into my head when I'm writing. Often, I approach the text without a clue of where I'll go with it. But as with so many creative pursuits of collaborating with God, we take the first step and He helps us to continue. As with the Israelites wandering through the desert, who had enough food for the day, He provides just enough inspiration for the devotional we're writing.

Try to develop a thick skin

The first publication I wrote for had an exacting readership. Any theological matter I addressed could be questioned; any uninformed opinion taken to task. I came to dread the letters from readers as they pointed out where I was lacking. But the readers' letters made me welcome my editor's comments all the more, for she knew her readership and helped shaped my voice through her edits.

Then I wrote a series on being a pilgrim in a foreign land. Bulky packages from the publisher started to pop through my letterbox, and this time I was amazed as the readers wrote with their stories of feeling in exile. The publisher said they'd never had such a response in terms of feedback. I felt overwhelmed with gratitude, made all the sweeter by my long history of not-so-easy letters.

Develop a team of early readers

Knowing you have people in your corner to talk through your work before submitting or publishing it means that you can more easily silence your inner critic while writing your first draft. If you're way off base, your early readers will let you know. They are your safety net, which means you can be freer with your jumps and tricks on the high wire. Being an early reader for other writers will also improve your own writing.

In closing, imagine with me how God might use your devotional writing to encourage someone in their journey with Him. You might receive an amazing letter, like I did, or you might not. We don't always know how God uses our words in the lives of others. But we know that He has the grace and ability to make our reflections to be words 'fitly spoken', 'like apples of gold in a setting of silver' (Proverbs 25:11, ESV). I pray you'll continue to craft these words in partnership with the Holy Spirit to speak grace, love and truth into the lives of others.

Amy Boucher Pye is a writer, speaker and retreat leader. The author of Seven Ways to Pray *(SPCK) and* Celebrating Christmas *(BRF), she writes regularly for the globally recognised* Our Daily Bread *and others, including* New Daylight *(BRF) and* Inspiring Women Every Day *(CWR). Find her at amyboucherpye.com. This chapter has been adapted and expanded from a blogpost on her website published in 2015.*

Using Your Story in Your Writing

Claire Musters

It may be that you have always known that you wanted to use your own story in some form of writing, be it a book, article, guide, devotional, etc. Or perhaps, like me, you had no idea that it would be something you would eventually feel stirred to do.

I started my career as a book editor, and I still edit both books and magazine articles, but then began writing when a publisher asked me to write a book because the manuscript that had come in was not good enough. The first books I wrote were on subjects that didn't include my own story. I am a Christian non-fiction writer, so often my books involve a devotional or study guide aspect to them.

I can still vividly remember the moment when I felt my writing focus was going to shift to be much more personal. I was sitting in a leadership training course, in a session on preaching. My brain had turned off somewhat, as at the time I didn't do much preaching so I didn't feel it was that relevant to me. And that's when I had one of the few times of hearing God speak to me via thoughts in my mind. I felt Him say that I would be speaking about my own story, but that I needed to write it down first.

That began a huge journey for me, which was a massive learning curve. First, what He had asked me to write about was what I would view as the most shameful aspect of my past. However, He has redeemed it, stopped me from being ashamed and it has since been the starting point of a book (*Taking Off the*

Mask, Authentic Media, 2017) that has shaped my ministry and working life since it was published. It wasn't an easy journey to get the book published, however, even though I edited for many of the Christian publishing houses. I kept getting the same response: your writing is great; we think the subject is good too – you just don't have enough of a platform. It took me two years to get a publisher for that book. Somehow, God had set a fire in my heart that burned throughout that time, and caused me to keep going, despite the knockbacks.

Since then, authenticity has been a real passion of mine, and I've found that a lot of the books that I have written in recent years include parts of myself in a way that my earlier writing didn't. I think it can really help the reader to trust you and what you have to say if you are willing to be vulnerable about your own life.

Deciding how to use your own story in your writing

It is important to be clear about why you feel led to use your own story. In *Taking Off the Mask*, for instance, it comes at the beginning as it was the start of my own journey looking at why we can hide behind masks rather than being honest. I hadn't actually put it upfront when I wrote the first draft. I had interweaved bits and pieces of my story throughout the book, until an editor who I really trust told me that it needed to be first and so I reworked the whole thing.

The beginning of the book now tells of the difficulties we had in our marriage – my husband was never home, owing to his job, and I really struggled with that. My own 'mask' was a victim mask. I learned, over a number of years, and through counselling both individually and with my husband, that there were a lot of underlying issues. Since then I've discovered so many others have similar issues with hiding who they really are, out of fear of rejection, cultural influence, upbringing, shame and guilt.

So I start that book with my story – as that editor pointed out to me, I think when you are dealing with issues like shame, disappointment, etc, people need to feel a connection with you. Then I look at the wider issues of why we wear masks – and other people's stories are woven into those chapters. In this instance, my story is the launching pad for unpacking a much bigger subject and, while I weave in lessons I have learned, the narrative isn't formed by it alone.

My most recent book is one about marriage, *Grace-filled Marriage* (Authentic Media, 2021), which I have written with my husband. We start this with a couple of chapters updating our own story (especially as I'd had feedback from readers that they wanted to hear his perspective about the circumstances I'd shared in the previous book). But then our experiences are simply interwoven throughout the narrative, wherever we feel it is pertinent to provide a practical example. But we don't just use our own story; we have asked others who we know have experienced things that we haven't, such as chronic illness and infertility, and so there is much more from other people in this book.

Sometimes life's circumstances may impact a writing project in a way you didn't expect. At the start of 2020, I was writing a thirty-day devotional on disappointment and loss when I got the call to say that my mum was nearing the end of her life and I needed to drop everything to be with her. Part of me had thought that that could happen, but I had never envisaged what followed – ten days of intense, deeply personal writing next to her bedside as she journeyed to be with Jesus. I know that God has called me to be open about some of the most vulnerable aspects of my life, which is why I have shared such deeply personal moments. That may not be your calling at all – it is important to be wise about what we do share and what we leave out. I always try to follow the Spirit's leading, and also check with my husband so that I don't overshare!

Ensuring your writing is accurate

Whenever we are using our own story, particularly if it includes something that happened years ago, we need to be aware that our memories will have a particular bent. I do tend to sit down and write from memory, but I have always been a diary writer, and found I did delve back into my diaries and often discovered little details that I had forgotten.

At times that was quite painful, and I had to take some time out to do some extra processing. However, I also recognised I was now in a different place, which was encouraging too. It also revealed to me when I had remembered something slightly wrongly – as did checking with people I trust who were around at the time, such as my husband and, before she died, my mum.

Including others in your writing

We are not isolated individuals, and so our own stories will include interactions with others. Changing people's names so that they are protected is always a good thing to consider, although I wouldn't advise simply doing so and hoping that they don't recognise themselves.

When I've asked others if I can include details of their own struggles, because I think it would be really helpful to what is being discussed in a chapter, I give them the option of changing their name or not. Some are happy to keep their own name, but a few have changed them. It may be that I ask them to write that section themselves if it is telling a part of their story rather than mine, but illustrates a point better.

It is important to ask people's permission if you are using an illustration that involves them in some way. I have never had anyone say I couldn't use an anecdote, but it is important to be prepared for that response.

Getting your story out there

I know that marketing can be a challenge for many of us. Sometimes, if we are using our own story we can be even more reluctant to continually share news about our new book or other publication. However, it is important to remind ourselves of why we wrote what we did in the first place. If we truly believe that our book will help others and that our story has an important role in doing that, then why should we be wary of telling others when it is available?

If your story covers a particular area of interest, then try to get in touch with publications, charities and other networks who may well be interested in helping you promote your work. We have found that marriage charities have jumped on our book, as they are always looking for fresh material to recommend to couples attending their courses or engaging on their websites.

Top tips for using your own story

I'm going to finish by giving you a few pointers of how to go about starting the process of using your own story in your writing.

- **Decide on what the purpose is**. Is it a straightforward memoir, or do you feel your own story helps to illustrate a wider subject?
- **Plan, plan and do more planning.** Don't just sit down and write, otherwise the writing will be unwieldy. Remember: you don't have to use everything that has ever happened to you – stick to the point and be willing to cut out superfluous details.
- **Be open to critique.** Allow those who know you best to read and critique your words before you publish. I would include close friends and family who will know the details of your story, but also writerly friends who can help with

the overall structure and flow of the narrative. Sometimes we are too close to our own story and need that sort of honest feedback. It is then our choice as to whether we make any changes or not. Just be open to the possibility of needing to. The editing process can be a humbling one, but always remember it's about making your work the best it can be.

Claire Musters is an author, speaker and editor. Find out more about her at www.clairemusters.com.

Poetry Makes Us Better Humans

Geoff Daniel

What makes us human? Well, writing poems for one thing, and everything it requires of us: intensely living, observing, thinking, using language, shaping and sharing our vision in particularly compelling works of art. Here are some suggestions for how to go about it, and in so doing, to make more of our God-given talents.

Get organised

First, collect the tools. Marshal your paper/pen/pencil/rubber. Shut the door. Silence your phone. Make time: get up early, or stay up late. Ensure your computer works and you know how to get the best out of it. Then, look, listen, think; undertake regular observation of and reflection on the world. Keep a notebook handy, and jot down words, phrases, possible lines, topics as they come up. Return to the book and use these ideas. Think like a writer who sees possibilities in everything.

Generate material

Try writing continuously on any subject, in a stream of the words that come to mind. Work from different stimuli: pictures, memories, news items, objects, lines from other people's writing, backs of cereal packets… anything will do to start the process. Don't pause to think hard, or worry about spelling, handwriting, etc. Just get words on the page; enjoy them. Then *select* interesting ideas, or good-sounding lines, and develop these. Throw nothing away – it's all grist to your mill. Once you have something working on paper, transfer it to the computer so you can redraft more easily. Try fitting one idea per line.

Be usefully self-critical

When you have something to work with, apply some key principles.

- **Does it communicate the idea?** Don't assume that readers will understand you or see your vision unless you help them. Read your words from someone else's point of view.
- **Interrogate each word.** Does it pull its weight? Was this the first word you thought of? Is there a better one? Is it there to impress, or does it do a real job? Is it deliberately 'poetical', or is it the real language of contemporary use?
- **Read it all aloud.** Does it flow? If it doesn't, does the irregularity add anything? Many poets recognise that poetry is the nearest that language gets to music. So think musically about your writing – staccato, adagio, allegro, crescendo, diminuendo, etc.
- **Does it appeal to the senses?** Think of touch, taste, smell as well as the more obvious hearing and seeing; appeal to the visceral. Make the reader feel it. Beware of abstraction and Big Words, like, 'My soul is…'
- **Question your technique.** Do you need to use rhyme? (No, you don't, actually…) If you have used rhymes, have they forced you into saying what you don't really mean? Are you overusing alliteration, imagery, etc?
- **Consider line and verse breaks.** Do they make sense? Do they add anything?

- **Shorten your work.** Be brutal; axe the weakest bits. Does that help?
- **Lengthen it.** Expand, let yourself go in detailing and developing. Is that better? Try doing the opposite of what you usually do.
- **Value accuracy.** Develop correctness of spelling, punctuation and grammar. Present work properly; follow conventions.
- **Question the authenticity of the poem.** Return to the experience, the object, the centre of the poem. Ask: is this writing true? Does it say what you meant? If not, are you happy with what it says now? (Things can reasonably change in the writing and unexpectedly new directions emerge.) What will a reader take away after the reading is done?
- **Rewrite your poems in different forms.** Experiment. Enjoy it. (Remember: it doesn't matter if it fails.) And then…
- **Put your poem away for a week** and return with fresh eyes to interrogate it.

Research

While you are working on your own material, feed your experience and understanding. Read other people's writing and learn what they understand and appreciate, what seems to work. Find out which poems by which writers are generally admired, and try to understand why. Read books, log on to websites, listen to podcasts; find out about poetry that doesn't naturally appeal to you, or you don't understand. Read anthologies, and 'How to do it' books. Learn the technical skills of poetry, and don't believe that spontaneity is the sole hallmark of 'real' poetry. Explore different forms: find out about villanelles, tanka, iambic pentameter…

Join a group/find an audience

Don't try to do it alone: engage with others. Obviously, in the COVID situation, writers' groups, the traditional way of meeting and sharing, were out. In their place, however, was a huge variety of online experience.

As an experiment, I recently googled 'poetry websites' and found a post offering a list of eight 'proven websites to read and share your poems on'. So, randomly selecting one of those, 'AllPoetry', which claims to be the world's biggest site for sharing poetry, I signed up as a (free) member. There is much on offer: dozens of special interest groups (331 at last count); many ongoing competitions on equally diverse subjects; and the opportunity to post your own poems, comment on others' work, and to buy resources, direct criticism and enhanced membership. I have had a number of interactions so far with other writers, mostly brief and restricted to pleasantries – supportive 'high-fives' seem to be the usual currency, although you can opt to join critique groups, too. I have researched what users say about this particular site, and find mixed responses: many are enthusiastic, noting the opportunities they have gained from interacting with other writers; others, however, have warned that the site can suffer from the downsides of all social media: superficiality, abuse and extremism. I would say on balance that it is worth exploring this type of online opportunity, while keeping your mind open, your expectations realistic and your guard up.

If you can find more personal and more local connections – ACW groups, for example, as advertised in our magazine, or church, or local educational centre-based groups – you may make more useful connections, who can help you to grow.

Find critical friends

Talking of growing, I think it helps writers to hear considered opinions from others who are not primarily concerned to protect your feelings or bolster confidence. It can help to hear from someone who says, 'I like/don't like this because...' or, 'Instead of X, why not try Y?' You can access such criticism through publishers, writers' websites and organisations like ACW. It will cost you varying amounts of money, and you should be clear about what you will be paying for before you agree. Be warned: criticisms are likely to come unvarnished, although informed, practical and sympathetic, one hopes. We try to help, even if it hurts a bit...

Competition

Entering competitions is another way of stimulating your creativity and offering potential exposure. I continue to do it because I find them a useful focus and challenge. Be aware that most competitions have very specific rules about things such as length, topic and what kind of presentation is required. You won't be able to communicate with judges, or change your entry after you have sent it in, and you won't get it back. Ignore these rules at your peril – it could be a waste of an entry, and an entry fee.

Performance and publication

At the time of writing, there is not much useful to be said about what used to be a thriving live performance scene, pre-COVID. However, 'Open Mic' and 'Poetry Slam' sessions will undoubtedly return one day. Google these to find out more – they suit a very particular type of poetry, but not all.

If you want to go further with your work, beyond the writing and the sharing of it with others on an informal basis, you might want to consider wider print publication. There are many options now but, perhaps inevitably, fewer chances of producing the traditional slim volume of poems, produced and distributed to high-street bookshops, all paid for by a publisher who has been so impressed by your work that they are prepared to take financial risks. You will need a consistent and impressive track record in winning competitions and publication in small poetry magazines/websites/events before anyone will consider investing in you – so explore these first. Self-publishing is always an option, and if you have the money, you will find people willing to produce a volume of your work and even market it for you. The line between self-publishing and vanity publishing has never been more blurred, of course. Just be aware of what it is you are getting into, and what product and services you will be buying. (And ask yourself this: would it be your talent and the quality of your writing that makes this book happen, or your cash?)

So – there they are: a few suggestions to help you on your way. Where to? Who knows what end can be achieved with a little time, effort, thought, courage, resilience, open-mindedness and ambition...

Enjoy the journey, traveller, poet, and – wonderful human being.

Geoff Daniel is the ACW poetry adviser.

Writing Historical Fiction

C F Dunn

Thinking about writing historical fiction? Have you been inspired by a teacher, a book you read, or a visit to a place that sparked a desire to dwell in the past? Or perhaps you have a family story to recount, or a social injustice to expose. You might wish to write about the famous – or infamous – or about the invisible many who form the backbone of history. Some novelists use history to paint a particular narrative, others as part of a time-slip novel, mixing and matching timelines. Perhaps you do not want to write about anything factual at all, but to use history as a backdrop to a fictionalised past where your original characters play out the drama of their lives. The past is your stage and time yours to command.

The ingredients for a historical novel are like any other, comprising characters, setting and language all wrapped up in a plot. The big difference is that the novelist cannot assume the reader's prior knowledge of the period or region in which the story takes place. Whether set fifty years ago (the point at which a novel might be deemed historical) or a thousand, a reader will need to be transported to that time and place. Do this by paying attention to period detail – moss growing in thatch, the astringent smell of coke fires, loose lacing on a woman's gown, and by referencing common human experiences – dusty furniture in a shaft of sun, summer rain on damp turf, a baby's cry.

Against such detail can be drawn specific historical events: medieval battles, Second World War air raids, fleeing refugees. Even if the story contains no historical events or characters, period detail will provide the authenticity of setting in which your story will thrive. Think of it as a favourite coat, one that fits in all the right places without chafing. A story should sit comfortably in its setting so that the characters are part of their world, and the world part of them. A knowledge of that world is highly desirable, but you do not need to be an expert in it to pull off a believable tale.

Use language in dialogue and prose to evoke period. To a degree this is a matter of personal choice – with a few caveats. Readability is all important. Whether you include contractions (don't, can't, won't) is up to you, as is throwing in 'thee' and 'thou', but these need to be used judiciously or they become self-conscious. Dialogue must appear natural to us, even if it would have been alien to a ninth-century contemporary. Something as simple as altering sentence structure can change the way it sounds. Avoid – like the pestilence – anachronistic words and phrases that jar. A wrongly placed word can jolt the reader and pop the fictional bubble you have so carefully constructed. An etymological dictionary is helpful here, as is the cautious use of the internet. Equally, comrade, the inclusion of certain words can transport the reader to a specific time and place. Use your novelist's head. Just because a word existed in the year 1500 does not mean it will sit easily in the twenty-first-century mindset. Many readers like to learn new words but will not want to reach for a dictionary every other sentence. Flora and fauna, too, can be dependent on region and time: you wouldn't have seen a grey squirrel in England in the fourteenth century. Remember, also, that what would have been a common phrase in the sixteenth century might now be inappropriate or even cause offence.

In the same way, tread carefully around sensitive topics. These might include matters of race and religion: apartheid in South Africa, the Troubles in Northern Ireland. Just because something is historical does not make it any less of an issue to some people now. History belongs to everyone, but to some it is not a collection of facts and a ready story, but living issues that affect the life they lead today. In that respect, historical subjects are not a free-for-all. Be mindful of it. If you do encounter criticism, listen, reflect and learn from the experience.

Great – you know the period, you have the place, but who populates it? Here you have a choice between original characters – those of your own imagination – or characters based on known people, or both. Let's have a look at these options in more detail.

The original character is your creation and your puppet, but acts within the confines of their world. Know their world – understand the time in which they lived, the expectations that might be placed upon them by society, their family, the religious institutions of the day. Be familiar with their daily routines: what can they smell, see, touch, taste? Did they eat flat bread? Rice? Noodles? Is your character a leader or a follower and, if the latter, do they follow out of duty or conviction? Who are their friends and who their rivals, and why? Your original character is your own, but that feisty gal in the thirteenth century who backchats my lord is breaking social norms and would probably earn a beating from her sire or dame. Breaking with norms had consequences; by all means explore them, but do so knowingly and with intent and with an understanding of the times in which your character existed.

Writing about known people is another matter. For a start, do you write as historian or novelist? And how far is it permissible – or wise – to blur the lines and deviate from received knowledge when bringing your story to life? The past is fraught with pitfalls. It goes without saying that while facts are incontrovertible, opinion is just that, and no two readers will agree on all points. How can they, when each is the sum of their knowledge, experience, expectations and culture in the same way as the people about whom we write? Take, for example, George, Duke of Clarence, he of the butt of Malmsey notoriety, to whom Shakespeare referred as 'false, fleeting, perjured Clarence'.[26] When it comes to his personal characteristics, there are a lot of gaps to fill. Nowhere in the historical record does it actually say that George was a good guy, a likeable chap, a jolly decent fellow; nor will you find mention that he was a dragon-slayer, a wife-beater, a drunk. These are opinions based on very little and sometimes nothing at all. With such sparse information it is up to the novelist to imagine their character. How this is done is down to what the writer is attempting to achieve and how far they are willing to go to achieve it. Yet we have a responsibility to the people of the past to represent them fairly. This does not mean erasing culpability for wrong actions, nor attributing positive characteristics we are fairly certain they did not have, but they were people for all of that and deserve to be treated with respect.

As for things we do know, I would argue that changing facts such as dates and events to suit the story is best avoided. There is no point in having George in Bristol sousing herrings on such-and-such a date when he was known to be in Bath pickling onions instead. As novelists it is up to our ingenuity to mould the story around the facts, not the other way around. Play about with history at your peril; there will always be someone who finds the obscure flaw in your facts, no matter how careful you have been. When it is pointed out, as it will be, acknowledge the error gracefully and move on.

We do, however, have scope to develop a character according to the needs of the story. Within reason.

Avoid slipping into the trap of using historical characters to make a moral point, using the badness of one person to amplify the goodness of another. Historic individuals were as complex and multifaceted as we are. They were not dependent on anyone else for their characteristics and, although influenced by others, their actions – ultimately – were their own, whether taken independently or under duress of circumstance. They craved

---

[26] William Shakespeare, *Richard III*, Act I, Scene IV.

cheese and disliked cabbage, had phobias, hay fever, a persistent cough. They might be frightened of dogs but adore cats, hide nutmeg under their pillow against cramp, or touch wood for luck when they think no one's looking. In bringing the past alive we resurrect those who lived it, not as pawns in a historical landscape to be moved around at the novelist's will, but living, real people whose stories will endure in the pages of the book you are about to write.

With a background in medieval history and specialist education, C F Dunn is an award-winning novelist of history, mystery and suspense. Find out more at cfdunn.co.uk.

Writing for Children

Cherith Baldry

Why do you want to write fiction for children? If you think it's easy, if you intend to knock out a couple of children's books to gain experience before moving on to the 'proper, important' novels for adults, think again. Writing for children is hard; children are fierce critics and are not at all reluctant to express their opinions.

And please don't embark on a career as a children's writer to make money. For every J K Rowling there are hundreds of humble, honest writers who are doing it for the love, and maybe earning enough in other ways to be able to go on doing it. So don't give up the day job!

Another reason for wanting to write for children is to teach them: maybe about general issues such as the environment, or issues affecting children, like bullying in school or problems at home. There's nothing fundamentally wrong with this, but remember that as a writer you are not a teacher; you are a storyteller. Your message has to be embodied in an exciting story. Paradoxically, your readers will assimilate it much more readily than if you had presented it to them directly.

The message Christians want to convey is the good news of our Lord Jesus Christ. But including Christian content in children's fiction has its pitfalls, depending on whether you are writing for a Christian or a secular market. Christian publishers will no doubt have guidelines about how much overt Christian content they prefer. Even for a Christian audience, I don't feel that there should be much – if any – straightforward preaching or quoting from the Bible, especially if this comes from adults towards children. It works much better if the Christian teaching is embedded in the story by Christian characters living their faith. I'm also not fond of stories that show a character's problems immediately solved if they become a Christian; if we look around at the real world, we know this is not so. A story can better embody a Christian message when it shows characters strengthened by their faith to cope with their problems. But as I said above, the story has to carry the message; the message won't carry the story.

Specifically Christian books are most likely to be read by the children of families who are already Christian, to bolster their faith. This is valuable work. But when writing for the secular market, it's sad but true that very little that is openly Christian will get past the editors. The comment will probably be something like, 'Don't make it too religious.' It is possible to include Christian activity as part of the characters' daily lives. But more importantly, I firmly believe that when a Christian is writing a secular story for the secular market, their Christian values will shine through.

So, having decided to write children's fiction, having chosen your approach and having a story in your mind, how do you proceed?

It's helpful for a children's writer to have access to children. Many of us have lovely, nostalgic memories of our own childhood, but the world has moved on. If you don't have children, grandchildren, nieces or nephews of your own, or if you don't work with children, then consider helping with Junior Church, or becoming a classroom assistant in a local school.

Another vital area to study is contemporary children's fiction. Haunt your local bookshops or libraries, but be careful to look at the date of publication. Use websites like Goodreads and study publishers' catalogues, which should all be available on their websites. We love the books we read as children, and some writers, like C S Lewis, seem as if they will go on for ever, but if Lewis were aiming for publication today, he would probably be writing differently.

Contemporary fiction reflects the real world. Two-parent families with 2.4 children and a dog are no longer the norm in this country, and whatever we feel about that as private individuals, as writers we have to reflect reality if our books are to be set in the real, present-day world. We see around us a variety of ethnicities and nationalities, one-parent families and blended families, children with disabilities or learning difficulties. Some of this needs to find its way into our books, but please don't trowel it in so your book becomes a kind of checklist of all the difficulties of modern society.

To some extent you can sidestep these problems if you choose to write science fiction or fantasy. In this case you can invent your own society, but it still needs to draw upon the real world. For almost twenty years I have been involved in the series *Warriors*, aimed at older children, about the adventures of clans of feral cats. I found this incredibly liberating. Because our characters are cats, we can deal with serious issues like the conflict between parents and children, the death of friends or family, falling in love with the wrong person, stories of friendship and betrayal, or times when courage is tested to the limit. Taking the fantasy route is not escapist; really good fantasy reflects the real world and sends the reader back better able to cope with it.

Children have three main requirements in the books they read. They want excitement; they want humour; they want interesting, lively characters that they can engage with. In children's fiction, it's essential that the child characters take the decisions and move the action along. Adults, like parents and teachers, must take a step back. This is one reason for the high mortality rate among parents in earlier children's fiction, such as Frances Hodgson Burnett's *A Little Princess* and *The Secret Garden*. It also partly explains the popularity of the boarding-school story – which may be experiencing a revival following the success of the Harry Potter books – since the school setting gives the children opportunity for independent action. It's tempting to portray children in a secure environment cared for by parents who make sure that nothing serious ever goes wrong, because that is what we wish for our own children, but it doesn't make for good fiction. Stories thrive on problems, difficulties and danger – geared to the age of the characters and also of the child readers – with characters stretched to their limits in coping with whatever the writer can throw at them.

The current publishing climate tends not to differentiate between books for girls and books for boys, though there are some authors, for example Jacqueline Wilson, who lean to one side or the other of the gender divide. A book will have the best chance of acceptance if there's a range of characters of both genders. And remember what I said earlier about keeping up to date. We don't live in the 1950s any longer, where the boys save the world while the girls make sandwiches and cry a lot. It's never a good idea to forget about, or offend, 50 per cent of your target audience; your girl characters should be just as brave, resolute and inventive as the boys. Both boys and girls can have weaknesses, too; boys are allowed to be frightened or to make mistakes.

Related to characterisation is the use of viewpoint. Using first-person viewpoint, where the main character is 'I', or third person, where you view events through the eyes of your main character, brings the reader closer to the story and helps to develop the character. Narrator viewpoint, where the story is told by the writer who knows everything, is more remote; in my view, it's hard to use successfully. And using your narrator to comment on the story and address the readers directly is now considered rather old-fashioned.

Each character should have an individual, lively speaking voice. And as well as showing character, good dialogue adds variety and pushes the plot along.

Think, too, about the structure of your story. Get your plot moving quickly, not necessarily with violent action, but with something interesting. Don't waste time introducing your characters and the background; drip-feed this information into the story as the action unfolds. Each event of your plot should arise out of the one before, building up to a climax where the issues are resolved. And though it's nice to see characters rewarded for their efforts, don't spend too long over this. Unfortunately, events we might enjoy if we were to take part in them don't make for the most interesting reading.

Finally, a word about language. Even for the youngest children, language doesn't have to be simplistic; you're not writing a reading scheme. Your choice of language can be vivid and challenging, bearing in mind the likely level of understanding of your readers. Remember that in writing for preschool children, and even the younger school years, you can assume parental help.

I began by asking why you want to write children's fiction. In the end, there's only one real answer: a children's book is the best way to embody the story you want to tell, and you are passionate about telling it. I wish you all the success in the world.

Cherith Baldry was a teacher until she took up writing full-time. She has published a number of children's books, most recently as part of the Warriors *team writing as Erin Hunter. She also writes adult mystery novels.*

Page to Stage

David Robinson

'All the world's a stage …'[27] At least that is according to another certain Midlands-based playwright. He could well have a point: we all have stories to tell, dramatic or mundane. Just speak them out loud and imagine them being told from the hallowed platform at the RSC, and life and colour will come cascading through your words. It is a wonderful if yet a somewhat apprehensive moment when your written words are spoken publicly on stage for the first time. Your hope is that they represent you well and do your characters proud. As Hamlet famously instructed his players, 'Speak the speech, I pray you, as I pronounced it to you, trippingly on the tongue …'[28]

Performance writing is very much associated with dialogue and not description. And when I indicate dialogue, I mean more the conversation you have with your audience and not necessarily with the fellow actors. Indeed, you may well have written a monologue or a performance poem. But consider how the King of the Diddy Men, Ken Dodd, once famously responded after being asked if it was lonely being a solo comedian all his life: 'Lonely, young man?' he quipped, 'I've had a fifty-year successful double act with my audience.'[29]

And that is really Act I, Scene I and line one. Put yourself in the stalls as you write, begin to listen as though you were sitting

---

[27] William Shakespeare, *As You Like It*, Act II, Scene VII.
[28] William Shakespeare, *Hamlet*, Act III, Scene II.
[29] During an interview at the Slapstick Awards in Bristol, 2016.

there in the middle of Row H, with a box of chocolates and clutching an overpriced programme. When you begin to write scripts and performance pieces, it is vital that you begin with the realisation that you are selling the piece to a reader who can hear and see your words. I don't need to know about the size of someone's hat or the variety of green shades in their coat, because I can see them. However, a conversation about how much the coat was, and which fashion boutique it was bought from and who it is intended to impress are all worthwhile additions to the opening scene. Remember all can be seen and heard just as the curtain rises and the lights fade up, and the audience takes in the scene and the characters, and their costumes. Including the green coat.

The characters tell the story, not the narrator, not the writer, but your collection of wonderful characters. You need to trust them and believe in them implicitly. Personally, my style of dramatic writing is very much character driven: I spend more initial time researching and creating character types before I delve into plot and substance. It is a wonderful exercise to build character profiles for four or five contrasting characters, put them into a situation together and then sit with them (and your laptop) and make notes on how you imagine your cast of characters would react and indeed evolve in specific environments. For example:

- A caravan in North Wales, during a very wet Bank Holiday weekend.
- A less than enthusiastic attempt at parlour games at a Christmas gathering.
- An important meeting in which plans are needed for a significant anniversary for the town.

Create your character profiles, make them all as different as you possibly can, and then have fun writing them into the situations outlined.

A slightly more straightforward introduction to scriptwriting would be to endeavour to research some real-life characters from history, or indeed from present day, and to then put a couple of them into a believable scenario and see what might develop. Some years ago, I read all I could about a couple of my comedy heroes, Stan Laurel and Oliver Hardy; huge stars of Hollywood in the golden age of the 1930s. In the autumn of their careers, they became somewhat overlooked and forgotten, until someone had the bright idea of encouraging them to do a theatre tour of the United Kingdom. They did it, thinking quietly that indeed their best days were well behind them, but they were wrong, and they filled huge theatres up and down the land for many months. So I wrote a fifty-five-minute play about Laurel and Hardy and put them both in a rundown dressing room in the basement of a Victorian Manchester theatre. I had done the research; I knew my characters intimately and had their location; I just had fun with their dialogue. It became a reflection on friendship, and reminiscing, and regret and, of course, laughter. It took me in all sorts of surprising directions, and there was a wonderful sense of release as the two characters began to lead my writing down unanticipated avenues. This is where the fun starts. Run with it if you can; if it becomes 'another fine mess', you can always press delete.

It is a very useful and liberating exercise to try: pick two characters who would naturally be in the same orbit, choose a closed setting, do good character research and then write.

Examples for you could be:

- Queen Victoria and Charles Dickens
- Winston Churchill and Neville Chamberlain
- C S Lewis and J R R Tolkien
- Agatha Christie and Arthur Conan Doyle
- The Queen and Margaret Thatcher

Creating characters from your own imagination can be equally refreshing and fun. I heard a children's author and illustrator being interviewed about her writing process recently, and she indicated that she would draw her characters first on a large pad of plain paper, often in great detail, and it would be an exercise that could take many days. Then she would look at these illustrations of her characters for many hours until, from the pictures, stories would begin to evolve. It is a wonderful suggestion and one I am sure could be a brilliant writing aid for you, should you, like me, reach a 'blank page day'. Either begin to draw a character or two, no matter how amusing the result, or, if you are reluctant to sketch, then just write as much as you possibly can about the profiles of the characters in your piece. And then read and reread the profiles, or sketch and resketch your drawings. Slowly the evolution of your wonderful characters will begin, followed by your blossoming story. Characters are the engine, the driving force behind any dramatic writing. Never rush the creation of the character. You need to know the detail of their backstory, even if those sitting comfortably with their chocolates in the middle of Row H in the stalls never find out. The actors will benefit from your research, as will, in the end, your superb play. And, as that Shakespeare chap so aptly puts it in *Hamlet*, Act II, Scene II, 'the play's the thing'. He knew a thing or two. Play on.

David Robinson, the Other Midlands' Playwright, is the artistic director of the Searchlight Theatre Company. Find out more at www.searchlighttheatre.org.

Comedy, Script-writing and the Bible

Paul Kerensa

Things go wrong. We try to fix them. We realise we can't do it on our own.

That could be the story of the Old Testament, or a present-day sitcom.

I've been writing sitcoms for nearly twenty years (for other people, while my own ideas sit on a TV exec's desks or in forgotten corners of my hard drive). Part of the appeal of sitcom for me is the satisfying worldview it adopts. They're half-hour parables disguised as entertainment. When we're laughing, we're listening.

Depending on your translation, Isaiah 2:11 says the 'eyes of the arrogant will be humbled' (NIV), or 'lofty' (NKJV) 'human pride will be brought down' (NLT). Or perhaps Blackadder's arrogance will find its comeuppance, or Basil Fawlty's stubbornness will be his undoing.

From Jesus' rich fool (Luke 12:16-20) to *Curb Your Enthusiasm*'s grumpy Larry, via court jesters, Falstaff, Buster Keaton and *Friends'* spoilt Rachel, pride comes before a fall. We love watching familiar flawed characters grow and change the hard way. There but for the grace of God go we, the viewers, the readers.

In prose as well as on screen, stage or sound, our characters don't have to be likeable for us to relate to their problems (and they must have problems). If audiences engage with their dilemmas, if their flaws seem genuine, then we empathise as they try to navigate this crazy world.

Some sitcoms do 'ave 'em

My writing time is split between prose and screenplay (and tweets – I write too many of those). But whatever you write, I think sitcoms can offer a helpful trimmed-down approach to telling a tale.

Sitcoms are tight. Every piece of dialogue works hard to earn its place. In a drama, a baggy scene may be less exciting, but tolerated. In a comedy, if the audience don't laugh, they feel you've wasted their time. Look at the critical response to bad sitcom compared with bad dramas. Ouch.

I think of a three-legged stool: character, story, comedy. Every page, every exchange, maybe even every line should inhabit at least one of those three. A golden sentence might communicate character, move on the story *and* be funny: a perfectly balanced stool. That's rare, though. Some lines are just characterful and comedic – great. Other lines propel the story and show us character – that's fine too. If you're not gripped by a sitcom scene, maybe that three-legged stool needs a beer mat under one of its legs: character or story or comedy may be lacking.

Whatever you're writing, is each page filled with character? Is the story moving forward? If not comedy, is your own genre of choice leaping off each page?

Faulty powers

Most sitcoms move at a snappy pace. No time to take in the scenery (which is often wobbly, anyway; see *Fawlty Towers* for details). We have learning to do! Protagonists try and fail and try and fail, before realising they can't solve the problem via their old bad habits. Not only that, their human failings make things worse. Not coincidence but causality.

Captain Mainwaring, Frasier Crane, Mrs Brown… they're all weighed down by their instincts. They fib, cheat, gloat, bicker, and other verbs that fall under traditionally sinful behaviour. White lies become greyer. What started as saving face spirals into one huge cover-up. A library fine might spark a chain of events leading to fraud, robbery or who knows what – and there's almost always a lie involved. (Show me a sitcom without a lie in it, and I'll say that's a Dutch sitcom. My Amsterdam friend can't understand why British sitcom characters don't just speak the truth from scene one.) Ultimately, some authority figure (police, spouse, priest, date) rules on whether the hero passes the test. There might be egg on their face, humble pie may be consumed – it's all still banana skins and custard pies, though it's dressed up to be a bit more sophisticated.

Sitcoms generally end in hope, not despair. Our character may have learned something, or not, but the joy of a sitcom over a film is the chance to get it right next week.

It's not just about character, but characters: Basil would have a pleasant time on his own in that hotel. It's the guests, staff and spouse who stop him from reading a book while listening to Brahms. We must share this planet together – and a good comedy demonstrates that's not always easy.

Joking apart: comedy and tragedy

I think comedy is a good lens through which to view life. After all (literally, after all), Christians believe that life has a happy end. The Greek masks would have it that there are two forms: comedy or tragedy. The shape of the comic grin drops in the middle but ends on a high. Inversely, the tragic grimace has a high mid-point but ends on a downer.

I know which one I prefer. A comic lens doesn't deny life's tragedies, though, nor should it. Every dramatic moment matters.

It's true of my neighbour, who tells me of her terrible morning, spending three hours opening a jam jar that then fell on her foot and smashed. It's true of Mr Bean trying to find his watch in a turkey. It's true of heart-breaking moments in *The Royle Family*. Comedies are full of dramatic moments, as important to those experiencing them as Tom Hanks' beloved volleyball vanishing over the waves in *Cast Away*. Just ask my neighbour with her broken toe covered in shards and strawberry conserve (never open a jam jar in flip flops).

Comedy is a zoomed-out genre. Charlie Chaplin said, 'Life is a tragedy when seen in close-up, but a comedy in long-shot.'[30] A God's-eye view of creation, appreciating the bigger picture, means the audience can see what the actors can't. From the farce of *Noises Off* to *The Vicar of Dibley*'s giant puddle or Delboy's chandeliers, we get the best view in the house.

If these pandemic days have taught me anything, it's that you can't judge anyone else's story till you've walked a mile in their shoes, to totally mix my metaphors. In times of self-isolation and upturning of social norms, I've heard friends rightly complain they had too much free time, home alone and bored. Other friends also rightly complained they had *less* time than ever, claustrophobic in a house with two home-schools, two offices and a confused dog. Neither deserves the response: 'Well, you think you've got it tough.' Instead, we give their stories credit.

Every day can be a battle, and we look forward to looking back on such days. Time will be a healer. Then laughter can be the second-best medicine (after actual medicine).

Are your characters being served?

Dramatic writing can benefit from a healthy dose of comedy. If you don't write comedy, don't write it off. Your genre may be

---

[30] www.brainyquote.com/quotes/charlie_chaplin_102081 (accessed 5th March 2021).

serious, but your characters can come to life if they show their funny side. Humour shows vulnerability.

In what way could your characters be funny? The dry wit of a detective? A classic fool in a best-friend character? A self-deprecating grandma? There's humour in dialect too: a Cornish gardener will have a different comic voice from a Geordie oil-rig worker. The Westminster bubble was skewered by *The Thick of It*, just as the church weekend was brilliantly pastiched by Adrian Plass. One was swearier than the other (I'll leave you to guess which), but both hit very different funny spots.

I had a filmmaker friend who was, well, making a film. Budgets being what they are, he set his short film in a small house with a small family (in terms of quantity, not size). It was an intense drama, full of arguments, despair and eventually family love – but he put the audience through the wringer first.

We worked on the script and found an opportunity for some brief levity. About two-thirds of the way through, a breath of fresh air was needed – so we momentarily took the story out of the house. Like Chaplin said, that long shot was called for, a wider view to give us perspective. Drawing on a passing reference to a neighbour, we had her bring over a cake for this struggling family. About to knock, she hears an argument from within, so hesitates, then leaves the cake on the doorstep and retreats next door again.

I don't know that it was the perfect solution, but it added some lightness to a heavy situation. It also showed that someone was there to care for this family. The cake was a welcome gift, and so was this scene.

Perspective is a marvellous thing. In real-life 'funny' stories from my past – a doomed date, a scathing heckle or an embarrassing incident with an M1 traffic jam and a water bottle – they were tough at the time, but a bit of space and distance does them wonders. Comedy is tragedy plus time, they say.

And here's another equation for you…

The big comedy theory

Only a fool would try to give a mathematical formula for comedy, so allow me to be that fool:

$$x \simeq y$$

x nearly equals y. This thing looks a bit like that thing: Michael McIntyre's anthropomorphised spice cupboard, with each herb and spice exhibiting human qualities... Victor Meldrew going to answer his phone but picking up a dog. Del-boy's bar fall works because the gap looks like a bar – if there was an obvious space, the gag would fall as flat as he does. (It's worth adding, to paraphrase writer E B White, that analysing humour is like dissecting a frog – you might learn something but the frog dies. So don't expect to laugh at these.)

If this thing looks like that thing, then maybe this person's story can look like my story. Consider Victoria Wood's uncanny ability to replicate the lives of her audience, or Jerry Seinfeld's superb pinpointing of modern life's quirks, from supermarket queues to phobias of public speaking.

Observational comedy says, 'Oh, you do that too?' We laugh, together, because we've all been there. That's also why Christianity's the faith for me. It's the only religion to speak of God dwelling with us, where we get to have a personal relationship with the creator of the universe. Mind-boggling, isn't it?

If life's a comedy in wide shot, though, I don't think of an Almighty audience-of-one sitting on a planet laughing at us, eating popcorn. Because Christianity's not-so-secret weapon is Christ. You had to be there, they say. Well, Christ was there. God is not laughing at us, but crying with us: tragic tears, comic tears. Jesus wept (John 11:35) – that two-word Bible summary that says He's been there. (So we don't have to.)

Christianity has Chaplin's up-close tragedy and wide creator view, all in one.

(Fr)ends

This is all just my tuppenceworth. Disagree by all means. Here are three take-homes, anyway (you probably already are home). Three, because comedy's rule of three is a good one – introduce idea, reinforce it, subvert it with a punchline. Oh, and the Trinity. So three is a good number...

- **This thing looks like that thing.** What does your scene look like? Does the wedding reception in your scene resemble a children's birthday party or a warzone?
- **Write what you find funny.** Someone else will too. Be yourself; everyone else is taken, as they say. If each character can be themselves too, maybe you can find their funny side.
- **Jesus used humour.** If it was good enough for Him... Surely you can't hold a crowd on a mount without a little crowd-work. Plank in eye, anyone? Jesus communicated truth with metaphor and parable. We can follow Him and do the same.

So I plead for comedy, in every project, whether you're writing drama, non-fiction, children's, historical or memoir. A little humour can help lighten the load.

Let there be light entertainment! And God saw that it was good.

Paul Kerensa writes books, including So a Comedian Walks into a Church *(Darton, Longman & Todd, 2013), co-writes sitcoms including* Not Going Out *and* Miranda, *and runs regular online writing courses. Find him on social media for details.*

A Short Story: A Step into the Unknown

Veronica Bright

Someone throws a log onto the fire. A baby raises a hand as sparks dart upwards. In the warm glow, the members of the tribe turn their faces towards the storyteller, and a silence holds them in its grasp. Then he begins his tale.

We've come a long way since then, of course, but we still love to exercise our imagination. Think of a group of friends or colleagues in the pub, swapping stories, laughing over jokes. Think of two neighbours meeting on the bus, sharing the experience of an overworked salesgirl misjudged as extremely rude. 'And I said to her, I said...' Life is full of stories.

We know what a remarkable storyteller Jesus was. Some would say He was lucky, because other people wrote His stories down, and writing a compelling story is more of a challenge! I think that in the telling, Jesus included a lot more detail than we ever hear, and I'm fairly sure He used eye contact and subtle pauses to help get His message across.

When I was a reception class teacher, I found that the way to the children's hearts was through stories. We were part of a government initiative to provide a piece of fruit for each child every day, and the teacher was encouraged to join in. I would sit in my chair on the carpet and the children would gather cross-legged in front of me. Our favourite fruit was bananas. I would hold mine, unpeeled, up to my ear and pretend to phone somebody's mum or carer. There was always a silence as I told the person on the other end of my banana how hard their child had worked that morning, or how well they had done in some way. After I finished the first 'call', I was always inundated with small voices begging, 'Phone my mum,' or, 'Please, please, phone my mum next.'

The power of story relies on the power of the recipient's imagination, which children have in abundance. But we are all children at heart, aren't we? We all love stories.

The trouble for the writer comes when we try to write them down. Author Erica Verrillo says, 'The short story is an art form that requires fast efficient character development, a plot that moves at the speed of light, and an ending that sticks in your mind like a song you can't get out of your head.'[31]

I think most of us in the ACW want to write stories that say something important without seeming to preach, to draw people's attention to the positive things in life. In other words, we want to create stories that matter.

Keep on empathising

In 1895, Mary Torrans Lathrap wrote a poem called 'Judge Softly', in which she appealed to her readers to think kindly of another person, whoever they are and whatever they have done. It's from this poem that we receive the wisdom to:

> Just walk a mile in his moccasins
> Before you abuse, criticize and accuse.

During lockdown I was listening to a talk on YouTube by Catherine Askew, a leader of the Northumbrian Community, in which she spoke about singing old songs in new ways. I felt that

---

[31] Erica Verillo, 'Top 6 Online Resources for Short Story Markets', *The Writing Cooperative*, 11 May 2018, writingcooperative.com/top-6-online-resources-for-short-story-markets-81282a93f0b1 (accessed 10th March 2021).

this simple phrase summed up what we as Christian writers are trying to do – sing old songs in new ways.

One of the members of the Plymouth Christian Writers has the gift of making characters in the Bible come quietly alive. She often starts not at the beginning but partway into their story, making our minds chase questions. Who can this be? Where are we? I know Peter's wife doesn't feature heavily in the New Testament. In fact, apart from having a sick mother, we don't know much about her (Mark 1:30). But my friend's story was told from her point of view, and I felt I got to know Peter a lot better through her eyes – flawed, sometimes irritating, yet honest, well-meaning and forgivably human. Like we are, I hope.

Once I visited Nepal, and while we were staying in a village, one of the farmers died in an accident when his tractor hit a dip and overturned. We were told by our guide that he'd drunk too much rice wine. He left behind a wife and children. They were not going to survive on the farm without the father. I don't know what happened to them, but later I invented a story about the daughter, a student at the local school. She had to go and live with her uncle and aunt. She took her school shoes with her, shiny and black, promising her mother she would work hard and be good. Her life had been shattered by her father's death, and it was shattered again when her uncle refused to send her to school with his two sons because, he said, 'School is for boys.'

A story about unfairness and poverty. A sad and weary kind of song expressed in a tune of my own making.

Keep on learning

Michelangelo was born in 1475 and lived for eighty-eight years, in an age where it was commonplace to die in your forties. Towards the end of his life, he is reported to have said, 'I am still learning.' What an inspiration!

In the twenty-first century, we have access to an overwhelming amount of knowledge. The joy of it is that if we want to write a story about a naturalist with a passion for proboscis monkeys in Borneo, we can find out all we need to know from reliable sources on the internet. Ditto an ornithologist searching for a spangled cotinga in the Amazon rainforests. Or we can investigate what exactly a professional mourner/golf-ball diver/animal care auxiliary does for a living.

More importantly, perhaps, we can commit ourselves to learning more about God, more about other people and more about how we can help save the planet. In this way we'll...

Keep on growing

If ever someone tells you that you're wasting your time writing stories not many people, if any, are going to read, do not let it bother you. Just look them in the eye, and say, confidently and quietly, 'We don't write to change the world. We write to change ourselves.'

Veronica Bright is a prize-winning author of short fiction and drama. She's good at daydreaming and gardening, which means her imaginative novel for children is nearing completion, and now it's just a case of getting on with the weeding and pruning bit.

Section Three

Filling the Bucket

Pandemic! My Historical Fiction Writing

Andrea Sarginson

Man of Glass is my first and only novel. It is set in 1349 in East Yorkshire as the Black Death reaches the village home of Amalric, a stained-glass window apprentice. After five years of writing and at the age of seventy-four years, I finally achieved the dream of becoming a published author in 2020... but it was the wrong time; *Man of Glass* was published just before the first COVID-19 lockdown. My novel was locked into isolation after only three book signings and hopes of more dashed. Set during a medieval pandemic, it turned out to be published as a modern pandemic simultaneously hit England. A novel irony!

Obviously, in terms of sales, mine is not a huge success story; on the other hand, what is success? When I look back, so much of my life was filled with things started and not finished, but my book is now testament to the fact that I did finish something and, what is more, it was a task I hugely enjoyed. As for being a Christian writer, I certainly didn't identify myself as one. I felt a call to write, but didn't recognise what or who called.

I discovered my need to write in 2011 and took an Open University writing course which was enormously helpful. I did well. However, rather than home study, I now wish I had done a course at a university or college where I would have had people to talk with about writing. I felt rather alone in my endeavours; it caused me to doubt myself and I've never really got over the difficulty of showing my work to people I know well – even my husband. However, joining a (secular) writing group helped. The leader criticised and praised my work at the correct level for me. It was a relief to find someone who, face to face, said I was a capable writer.

I began writing my novel with a pompous idea – to teach through my writing. My working life had included young adult and adult teaching, so it seemed a natural thing to do. I learned that there was a GCSE history module about 'medicine through the ages' and I thought I could write a story encompassing everything that needed to be learned for the exam; revision made easy, if you like. However, it was I who learned that too many facts obscure any hope of an interesting story. It is people and places that make past times live again. I abandoned the idea. I needed to shift slightly from the pattern of my working life to something new, and draw on my life experiences.

I clung to the medieval setting, though, and was inspired by a visit to a ruined, ancient village in East Yorkshire, Wharram Percy. Wandering around, I realised that each grass-covered, stony hump and the ruined walls of the village church held the mystery of people's lives. I also discovered that the Cistercian Abbey of Meaux had been nearby. Both church and abbey would have been strong elements in everyday life. In that visit I found an approximate location for my story and a developing plot.

I had two medieval themes. One was the first devastating wave of the Black Death, and the other stained glass – a burgeoning craft valued in many medieval branches of the Church but seen as decadent in others. The backbone of my novel thus took shape: a stained-glass window apprentice caught up in the first wave of a devastating pandemic. I started my research. Oh, the joy of unfettered rummaging in books and on the internet! From annals I found on the web, I learnt that Meaux Abbey had suffered both an earthquake and the Black Death in 1349 – a gift for my imagination.

As for characters, I looked at my own passions and revisited my previous studies and experiences from nursing, the Church and art history, especially stained glass. I explored the early glass of York Minster. It was all so fascinating that I was easily distracted way beyond my theme, and I realised that to move on I had to become more disciplined. I settled down to study only the relevant local history before and during 1349, that which my characters would have known. I studied how the Black Death may have been spread and the reactions of people to it, including those of the Church. I imagined the medieval world with its sights, sounds and smells. When I put my main characters into the mix, with their own loves and opinions, I had the germ of a story and could begin.

Plotting out the whole novel didn't work for me. I was happier to let my characters develop the story, to let things evolve as ideas came to me. The first page was hard and it changed many times. Eventually I started with the threat of the Black Death introduced in a tavern scene, followed by my main character suffering from a hangover. The creative process was really enjoyable.

Then came the reckoning. I had a finished novel that I wanted to be published, but had no idea whether it was good enough. I had to let someone see it. I baulked at the idea. In the meantime, while I didn't consider myself a Christian writer, I had done some writing for my church and had registered with the ACW. In the magazine I found a list of people who would review writing. I sent off my manuscript. This proved to be extremely useful – not that the response was very complimentary, but there was enough to make me feel it was worth carrying on!

Then I got into a muddle. I rewrote and sent the manuscript off to a general literary consultant, but the results of this unsettled me. The critiques took a long time to be returned, which was frustrating and, along with some very useful guidance, it was suggested I should introduce more suspense and spice. I made the plot a little raunchier by making the young apprentice desire a servant girl. The story lengthened. I felt I had done my best, but I had lost some of my enthusiasm.

I decided to go directly to a publisher. At this, I was a total innocent. One of the disadvantages of older age is that switching one's mind to modern communications and technology can be anathema. I tentatively emailed a few publishing houses but, I have to admit, I ignored all advice about how to get published. Then I looked at the ACW section advertising new books to see who the publishers were. I found the Christian publisher Instant Apostle. This was a light-bulb moment! My book was written from a Christian perspective – of course it was: I had included church window manufacture; church wall paintings; the Cistercian approach to art; the conflicts between superstition, medicine and the Church over cause and treatment; a significant character was a village priest, others were monks; Amalric and a physician struggled with their own faith against the magnitude of what they were facing. How had I not realised it was a story about Christianity?

I contacted the publisher. Much to my surprise, my manuscript was accepted. However, that was a new beginning, not an end. The first reader's report said in no uncertain terms that the raunchy bits had to go – much to my relief. Life experiences are valuable, but how far you wish to recall them is another! I revised happily and accepted that I was a Christian writer. I drew a plan of the medieval village and an illustration of Amalric's home and workshop, and wrote words for two songs based on medieval poetry. I received a lot of help from the publisher. I had a brilliant copy editor helping me get things right with my manuscript, others with the presentation.

Then came the amazing day when I received a pile of books: *Man of Glass* with a lovely blue stained-glass cover, but… it was just before the first lockdown of COVID-19! After assuming the *literary* Black Death pandemic of 1349, I found myself in an *actual* pandemic. Like in my novel, the world seemed to stop. Readers have asked me if I had a premonition, like an ancient prophet, when I wrote it. No, I did not.

Would I have chosen the same topic five years before if I had known a pandemic would loom at the same time as publishing? Yes, I would, because the book is about me as much as the characters I have invented. I had to write it. Also, the history is real and deserves to be told – we have suffered pandemics before.

As I start my second novel, a sequel, I'm better placed to understand both the technical and creative aspects of Christian writing. I can use the experiences of youth and older age. I can use my passionate interests and experiences. I must be true to myself and recognise my Christianity.

Andrea trained as a nurse, art historian and adult teacher. She also spent fourteen years as a reserve army nurse. Her interest in the histories of medicine, art and Christianity is the driving force behind her writing, which she took up in retirement. She particularly enjoys exploring the long relationship between artistic expression, healing and faith. Since 2012, she has been an Authorised Lay Minister in the Manchester Diocese.

How ACW Helped Me Go Places as a Writer

Annmarie Miles

I had heard of the 'M4 car park' but never experienced it. Now I understood the concept. We were on the M42 in motionless traffic. We heard more of our 'on the road' playlist than we'd ever heard in one go before. It was June 2018, and my husband and I were on the seemingly endless journey to Scargill House. I had seen the advertisement for that weekend on the ACW Facebook page and I knew immediately I had to go. I showed it to my husband and simply said, 'I need to be at this.' That evening we booked our places.

As we sat in the queue of cars, I was beginning to doubt we would ever get there. It gave me plenty of time to think as we inched our way northwards, and I thought back to when I had joined ACW in 2015.

We had just moved back to the UK from Ireland. Joining a writing group was high up the to-do list:

- Find somewhere to live;
- Find a church;
- Find work;
- Find Christian writers to connect with.

Did you know moving to a new house/country can play havoc with the muse? It felt like I'd put her in storage with the furniture. I was applying for jobs, sorting out bank accounts, getting proof of address paperwork, but I could not blog or even start a short story. I wondered if writing was leaving me. I was afraid that I was a writer in Ireland, but in the UK I would have to be something else for God. Then I found ACW on social media and immediately felt part of a community that loved God and loved words. Having left behind a large writing network in Ireland, this new family of writers was just what I needed to remind me how to put pen to paper.

My first ACW event was in Leeds. My husband booked us a hotel room and researched coffee shops where he could read his newspapers. I spent time choosing which notebook to bring and deciding which workshop to opt for. On that day I met, face to face, some people I'd only exchanged Facebook 'likes' with. During coffee time, some of us shared our hopes and dreams for writing, our successes and disappointments. I could do that at any writing day, but at this event everything was grounded in God's plans and purposes.

A couple of years later, I was on a Megabus to London to hear Glen and Emma Scrivener speak at the ACW day in London. I was reunited with writers whom I dared to call friends. During the Q&A panel, I popped my hand up to ask the question that made me sick in the pit of my stomach. 'What if it turns out I'm no good at writing?'

God sent me an answer that challenged me and blessed me. I remember walking up The Mall, heading towards Buckingham Palace, on my way to catch the bus back to Wales. Actually, I strutted up The Mall. Not in pride (honest), but in confidence, a renewed breath of God fuelling my steps and the words that were in my heart. I began writing what will probably be the work of my life, an examination of my love and hate of food, weight gain and weight loss; a story of how God spoke into my obsession with eating, for His glory.

I went on to write the book and it was saved in the depths of the laptop that sat on my knee as we crawled up the M42. I was excited about my first Scargill weekend. Adrian and Bridget Plass would be there. Nick Page would be there. I would be there, eventually. When we arrived at Scargill House, the event had started. I snuck in the back and someone gave me their seat. Adrian was in full flow and I was so excited to be in the same room as this man whose words I'd devoured as a growing Christian. The next day I spoke to Adrian in the queue for breakfast, and, when I thought things couldn't get any better, I later found myself sitting with Nick Page and his wife at dinner, talking about my *weighty* book. He was interested. He laughed at the title and encouraged me to pursue publication. I determined I would.

As we drove back down the M42 towards home on that Sunday afternoon, I was once again burning with enthusiasm, but also with fear. Fear that God might really want me to tell this deeply painful story, and that it could be more powerful than I'd ever imagined possible.

Now it is the beginning of 2021 and the work is ongoing. There is still lots to do. I have had some great feedback from people whose knowledge and wisdom I admire greatly, and once again I am challenged to take my writing to another level. But whether the book finds its way into readers' hands or not, God has used ACW to bring it into being. From my adopted home in South Wales, He brought me to London and then to Scargill and, in doing so, awakened courage to dare to hope that His own hand is not just on my story, but also on the telling of it.

I feel a part of my life has been stolen by years of being extremely overweight. I long to be free of it, and I truly believe writing the book is part of that process. Maybe it is no coincidence that this is a jubilee year for ACW. Could it be that I could find forgiveness for my gluttony? Liberation from my slavery to food? Rest from the exhaustion of the obsession with eating? Oh, that it could be true! God continues to use ACW to bless and challenge me, and I am privileged to be a member during this season of jubilee. May He bless the next fifty years, for all of us.

Born and bred in Dublin, Ireland, Annmarie Miles now lives in South Wales with her husband, Richard, in a home full of books, musical instruments and fridge magnets. She can be found at www.annmariemiles.co.uk.

From Reader to Writer

April McIntyre

I find it hard to call myself a writer. Bulky manuscripts tied with ribbon, feverish negotiations with publishers, book signings, fame and perhaps fortune have little to do with my quiet life and scribbling. Yet I have always been a word person, reading voraciously, composing little stories and rhyming verses from an early age and later discovering a gift for literary criticism, which led me to study English literature and then to complete a PhD. During my time at university, I kept the gremlins of anxiety at bay by writing long letters home – spontaneous, personal letters, full of new experiences, feelings and struggles, with little regard for spelling or grammar.

I became a Christian around age sixteen when I first realised that Jesus Christ was more than a historical or mythical figure. I encountered Him as the suffering Saviour but also as a friend I would travel with throughout the twists and turns of my life. Away from home, my faith grew, inspired by local student groups, churches and events, and instinctively I began to write my own psalms, poems and prayers. Occasionally I would send one of these in a letter to my mother, only to find, when I returned home, that she had read it to many of her friends from church.

It was much later, now married and settled in Derby and in the middle of training as an Anglican lay minister (reader), that something significant happened. We had been given an assignment to write on the doctrine of the Holy Spirit. This included writing a short piece for a parish magazine. I really enjoyed putting together this simple explanatory article, using clear section headings, everyday analogies and liberal sprinklings of clip art. 'Just a bit of fun,' I thought, until my marked assignment was returned. The assessor's comments were very positive, and he concluded by saying that, when licensed, I should make sure I used my talents to write for a parish magazine, website or perhaps for the Diocese. This was the tiny spark that illuminated a new phase of my journey.

Derby Diocese sponsors a weekly column called 'Faith Files' in the Saturday edition of our local newspaper. Various writers, lay and ordained, take it in turns to write about current issues, church celebrations and outreach, or personal spirituality. Back in 2008 I joined this team and found it an excellent discipline, writing in a way appropriate for a wide range of readers, with or without a faith, and working to a word count of under 300 words. This forced me to tighten my prose, avoid Christian clichés and jargon, and edit ruthlessly. Occasionally someone might mention that they had seen my piece in the paper, but feedback was minimal. It was like scattering seeds in the darkness, trusting that the Holy Spirit would blow a few to fertile ground where someone was in need of encouragement.

On one occasion, I received an email from a friend. Her father (not a churchgoer) had been reading his *Derby Telegraph* and come across my reflection about St Teresa of Ávila's famous 'bookmark' prayer. I had introduced this by describing the pleasures of opening up old books, never knowing what you might discover tucked inside, from pressed flowers to concert tickets or old photographs. The father read the piece to his daughter over the telephone, saying how moving he had found it. It turned out that he had recently lost his wife. Now he and his daughter had to face sorting through his wife's things, particularly her books. Suddenly, a task they had been dreading was transformed into a treasure hunt, connecting them with happier memories.

Through this experience, I began to see that God often works in ways we least expect. Here it was not the religious part of the reflection but the initial scene-setting that helped father and daughter take a step towards healing.

In 2008 I also signed up to be a book reviewer for the magazine of the Central Readers' Council, now called *Transforming Ministry*. This meant receiving several brand-new Christian books each year and writing reviews that would be relevant and helpful for lay readers. The word count for this was very tight but, drawing on skills from my old academic training, I was able to produce some interesting analyses on a wide range of topics.

In 2017 I joined Café Writers, the ACW writers' group in Derby. My last few years had not been easy, owing to ongoing health issues, medication changes and just getting older. I found it hard to concentrate, to process thoughts and speak to others. I was often frustrated and depressed. My old spontaneity in talking to God and journalling my thoughts had virtually dried up. Writing sermons and articles took so much longer, as if every word had to be wrenched out screaming.

The new Café Writers group came along at exactly the right time for me, providing inspiration and encouragement to experiment with different styles of writing. We had 'homework' to play around with, and opportunities to share what we produced with others. I really enjoyed this. I could see, by people's reactions, that there was merit in my writing, and they weren't just being kind, and I began to relax and feel I had a contribution to make. I owe a great debt of thanks to our resourceful and committed leaders.

As I write today, I still don't find it easy, but I am happy to work in miniature: writing short reflections, prayers and poems along with the odd sermon or book review. I write a regular column called 'Still Space' in our monthly church/village magazine, reflecting on how we can experience God's presence through the changing seasons, the Church year and everyday life. This is something I was able to continue throughout the

COVID lockdowns of 2020 and 2021, reaching out to those stuck at home, separated from family, activities and worship.

My journey continues onwards, taking me beyond parish and Diocese into a wider world. I have written pieces for the ACW Lent and Christmas anthologies, short reflections for BRF's international daily notes, *The Upper Room*, and several longer articles for magazines. Who knows where this path is leading?

It is a great blessing to write as a form of therapeutic self-expression, but what a privilege when we can share the treasures of God's Word and world with others, however we do that. Such gifts must be held lightly, even as we work hard to hone our skills, for we cannot possess, only use them. As we stare at another blank piece of paper, or empty computer screen, we are reminded that God's grace is sufficient for us because it is in our weakness that the nature of His power is revealed (2 Corinthians 12:9).

April McIntyre enjoys exploring spirituality and creativity, feeding her work as a lay minister in Derbyshire.

You Need to Write That Down

Carol Purves

'You need to write that down.'

As a youngster, whenever I told a story or shared exciting events with my friends, the advice was to write it down. My mother had some writing talent, so I probably inherited the ability I have from her. Publishing was so different in those days.

At secondary school, I had an English teacher to whom I related well. It became a subject in which I excelled. In the thirteen different jobs I had during my working life, I found excuses to write little poems and articles. I cringe when I look back at them now.

I had to retire from work in my mid-fifties because of ill-health, and that is when the writing 'kicked off'. I started by having letters printed in various women's magazines. At about £3 a letter, I felt I was earning a fortune. Invalidity benefit didn't pay much.

It was at this point that I started writing articles about historically famous people for *The Lady* magazine: Carl Bechstein the piano builder and John Cadbury of the chocolate empire, among others. It was a very different magazine in those days. This stopped when I submitted an article on the life of Gladys Aylward, the missionary in China. I believe her life story was too Christian for that publication.

By that time I had collected so much information about this missionary that I still remember saying out loud to myself, 'I've got enough information here for a book.' That's how it started. Many months later, the fourteenth Christian publisher that I submitted the manuscript to accepted it (Day One). With the three reprints of this book, I eventually earned enough money through royalties to fund (most of) a trip on the Trans-Siberian Railway. Heady days. It has been downhill since then.

Then I discovered the Association of Christian Writers and have been a member ever since. When I lived in the London area, around 2000, I was able to serve for a few years on the committee. I was so proud to be part of that.

My memory doesn't go back far enough to remember the association being called the Fellowship of Christian Writers, but I do remember when the magazine name changed from *Candle & Keyboard* to *Christian Writer*. I'm ashamed to admit that I was one of those who voted against the change. Well, it was a long time ago.

I will never forget the committee meetings we had at the Salvation Army meeting hall in Oxford Street, London. These meetings always took place on a Saturday, and when we left at about 4pm, the streets were so full of shoppers that I had to elbow my way to the underground station. Unladylike, but I was stronger in those days. The names on the committee list are different now, and some of the committee members I served alongside have been called to higher service. I owe them many thanks for their encouragement and training.

I was happy to join a local group, in southern Essex, and I'm pleased to say I am still in contact with a few of the writers from those days. Fifteen years ago I moved north to Carlisle and formed the Cumbria Christian Writers group. This gave me a new set of writing friends. Members come from west Cumbria, Hexham, Lancaster and over the Scottish border. Although we were meeting in Carlisle, for the last ten months, owing to the coronavirus pandemic, we have been having our meetings on Zoom.

I don't really do New Year resolutions, but at the beginning of 2020 I resolved to be more closely connected with the association, maybe get to the London meetings and times away at Scargill. At that time the words 'COVID-19' and 'lockdown' were unknown. What a difference a few months make! So that New Year resolution was moved to 2021 or beyond!

'You need to write that down.'

Before the lockdown I started on a book of reflections on life. My imagination was fired by true stories that my friends shared with me about their children and families. Every encounter I had with people gave me a few more ideas. With the arrival of the pandemic, contact with people became minimal, so ideas and inspiration dried up. I had written 42,000 words when I lost the lot. I mean really lost! My friend who helps with my computer couldn't come into the house, so had to support me remotely. This meant that although the work was retrieved, it had to be completely retyped.

Who says writing is easy? I have many lovely friends, but some think I sit at the computer and copy-type with no creative powers at all. When I announced I was having a four-day, self-catering, writing retreat alone at my house over the New Year, I received the comment, 'How lovely, you deserve a little holiday.'

Wiping the sweat running from my brow, flexing my frozen fingers and the same with my numb bum, I press on. 'Perseverance' is mentioned many times in the Bible. A message to all of us.

'Why don't you write it down?'

That is what I am endeavouring to do with the help of and thanks to ACW. I owe a great debt to the Association of Christian Writers. Thank you for all you mean to me, and the friendships I have found on the way.

At the time of writing, with this pandemic, another page is being written in our history. There are stories of Zoom meetings, nationally and locally. Because of our isolation, some members have taken to phoning writers in the Association whose friendship had lapsed. Eventually, with God's help, we will draw positives out of this time. Our writing skills and the message we bring are needed more than ever.

Carol Purves is the author of a number of books on Christian missionaries, with one book of daily observations on the way.

What Do You Want to Be Known For?

Caroline Greville

My journey into Christian writing began with things going wrong, namely my publisher for my nature memoir and PhD project hitting a major financial crisis and dropping all new writers. *Badger Clan* was suddenly without a home, and I sensed God was saying something to me again: 'What do you want to be known for?' I had had a yearning to write for God before then, but there hadn't been the opportunity. Yet now He was affirming what had been building in my heart for some time.

With old bridges burnt and the desire to concentrate on a new project at the fore, *Badger Clan* was finally independently published on Kindle Direct Publishing and soon found its way into Waterstones, with invitations coming in for me to speak there and at book festivals. Was I getting distracted? I don't think so, for the project needed a conclusion. It wasn't that I felt it was *wrong* to publish it, and my faith *does* feature in it – but just that God had other designs on my time and abilities. I no longer had a publisher waiting for a second nature book, and I could write what I wanted to at last. My agent had freed me up too.

So what did I want to be known for? 'Belonging to Jesus' would be my adamant answer, then as now. I knew He was asking me to make Him central in my work and that my identity would be as a Christian writer rather than a 'writer with occasional Christian themes'. My intention is to make Him better known and understood, whatever the cost. I want people to connect with Him, encounter Him in what I write, and even to find salvation.

My first opportunity came with the ACW competition to submit a story for inclusion in its 2018 Christmas anthology, *Merry Christmas Everyone.* I researched and wrote my story, 'Welcome, Little King', and another quickly followed. I enquired and was told only one story could be submitted per person, but that didn't matter; soon I was on a roll. I could even say that my first attempt was the small stone that tripped an avalanche of stories, the ACW invitation to write coming at just the right time. 'Welcome, Little King' was included in the anthology and by the time the anthology came to print, I had finished many more. A new project had begun. The end result is a series of interlinked short stories, based on accounts in all four Gospel narratives, researched with the aid of commentaries, works of art, websites and much prayer.

I found a traditional publishing contract over the course of one weekend, which felt very different from my first experience, and *Gospel Voices* was published by Faithbuilders during the first UK lockdown. 'Hoorah,' I should say. 'What an answer to prayer!' Yet it didn't seem ideal. It was slow to roll off the printing press, there were no book launches to go to, and it was much harder to generate publicity and support. However, I know that it is selling, and I'm heartened by the comments I've received. More than anything, I remain encouraged that it was a book the Lord wanted me to write, and I believe He promised that salvation would come from it.

Early on in the project I had a picture in my mind's eye of poppy seed heads bursting and spreading on the wind. It wouldn't leave me. On the day that I finished writing the last story, I stumbled across a mass of poppy heads ready to burst, and I found myself astonished. I think I've found some of that seed since, and in unexpected places. I now keep a letter tucked into my Bible from a lady whose lockdown life has been made much happier as a result of having *Gospel Voices* in her possession.

I have two pieces of advice for anyone wanting to write for Christian publication. First, start small and look for opportunities to receive exposure for your work. ACW groups give the chance for you to share your writing and receive both constructive input and encouragement. Look out for invitations to submit pieces to its *Christian Writer* magazine. Anthologies are always a good way of getting work 'out there' before a longer project is underway, and social media and magazines sometimes advertise, needing writers to fill their pages. Starting small really is the way to go, with you seeking homes for short pieces, and often. So many novels have their roots in short stories, and they are the best training ground – there's no need to wait until you have something much longer to run with.

My other piece of advice is to prepare well, not only in terms of research, but also in terms of enhancing your writing ability. It is honouring to God when we produce something good, and we can all get better by learning the tools of the trade, as we would with anything else we are new to. ACW puts on excellent short sessions regularly, and if you can spare the time, look into a creative writing course with your local Adult Education provider, or even a university in your area. I have the privilege of teaching at both, and can tell you that you'll become a better writer if you devote time to such training. I see the difference in my students. You'll also make lifelong friends – writing can be a lonely occupation – and your faith will spill out naturally in God-given moments over the weeks, months and years.

My final thought to leave you with is not advice, but a gentle reminder that we all need from time to time. It is this. As Christians we are writing for God's recognition, not our own. I expect that, like me, you'll find this a very freeing thing. The publishing world can be driven and competitive, but thankfully our God is not. Part of His aim for us is that we grow in the process of writing. As Christians we are able to go about His work, pen in hand, and it's really not just about how we reach others with this, but how God works in us as we write; we wear a golden life jacket and blow on a golden whistle, with Him protecting and sustaining us as we share and others hear. Christian writing without a doubt draws us closer to God, if we are going about it with the right motivations. Of course, He cares about our development as believers too, and if we can connect with Him on a deeper level through writing faith stories, then it has to be a good thing.

I do remain convinced that our assessment of writing 'success' can be too worldly; if one person comes to faith through what each of us writes, then it will have been worth it. If one person has a better understanding of who Jesus is, then it will have been worth it too. Imagine finding people in heaven who are there because you took the time to write something the Lord was impressing on you, something that had fired your imagination or moved your heart. I think there will be moments in eternity like this for all of us who follow through on the call God gives us.

Caroline Greville lectures in Creative Writing at Canterbury Christ Church University and is author of Gospel Voices; *her latest book is now out on submission in the UK.*

A Long Journey to Publication

Claire Ross

'If anything should happen to me, you will finish the book, won't you?' my husband, Alan, asked, as we drove over the hills of the Isle of Wight in 1996.

'How could I do that?' I queried. 'It is all about you and Finchden.'

'It's all there. The writing is done. It is more a question of getting it all in order.'

Rashly, I promised, little thinking I would really have to do it.

Six weeks later he went early morning swimming, as was his habit, and dropped dead as he ran around the pool after his swim. A heart attack.

In 1999 I retired, partly on health grounds, from my work at Royal Holloway, University of London, with the manuscript still consisting of 250,000 words, some in chapters, but much still in note form and scattered among his photographic and gardening notes. I would need some new focus to help me complete the task. For years I had been a supporter and user of the resources of the London Institute for Contemporary Christianity (LICC), and was delighted by the opportunity offered by its course for writers, staffed by members of the Association of Christian Writers, and led by Chris Leonard. It was a stimulating introduction to the experience of sharing what I had written at speed, with the variety of exercises and different genres to which we were introduced. It gave me confidence to join a writers' group, initially a postal group which operated for about three years.

Our ground rules were simple. We would look for what we could make comments about, and ensure there was more encouragement than criticism, although we would always seek to be honest. If the material was suitable for publication, we would make suggestions and not be at all offended if the recipient did not follow through. We would aim to pass material on within ten days. This would mean that our writing would come back to us after about seven weeks. That felt manageable for us all.

Contributions covered a range of genres and subjects, and that has always been one of the joys of ACW, whether at meetings, on courses or in a local group. The group faded as the initiator took a writing post professionally and had additional family responsibilities. For me, a health crisis intervened. About a year later, at an annual general meeting of ACW, I connected with a couple of members of the Bromley group and was invited to join them at their monthly meetings. The gatherings included, among others, a watercolour artist, poets, a biblical scholar translating commentaries, a couple of ministers' wives, a librarian, a community dramatist and a primary school teacher. Some were retired, others still in full-time employment and/or home based. It was mainly a female group but with men joining and sharing for various lengths of time. People came from the close proximity of Bromley and Hayes or as far as an hour's journey away.

I had started to tackle the task of organising Alan's book and the group members were supportive and encouraging, whether I brought some work on that or something quite different. The variety of contributions from them and their overall encouragement to think about publication, even if not pursued, was a good stimulus to keep editing and writing myself.

A writers' weekend at Scargill House, led by Adrian and Bridget Plass, was a major stimulus, and particularly emphasised the importance of prayer, guidance and consultation. The sense of community, of writers, and the wide range of people, was a joy; worship sessions and sharing meals truly reflected the community spirit in which Scargill excels. A discussion with a publishing agent, a member and a speaker at the weekend helped me focus on what I needed still to do with the manuscript.

Unexpectedly, my nephew, son of my half-sister, whom I had never met as she lived in Argentina, made contact, and his wife and I became good friends when she visited the UK. To my delight, she had proofreading skills and offered to work on the manuscript. Her comments and detailed suggestions were wonderfully helpful, but best of all, she loved the content. I was able to send the document electronically to two of the staff who had worked with Alan, and again received positive comments and suggestions. It underlined for me the importance of what I had learned through ACW about getting comments from others to help take a different perspective.

The manuscript was complete, and I wrote to the publisher who had originally encouraged Alan to write his autobiography. He had submitted an account of specific therapeutic work undertaken at Finchden Manor, a community instigated and led by George Lyward. The publisher took Alan out to lunch, told him that he wrote well but that his book was the sequel to the real story, which was how he, Alan, had been at Finchden Manor as a boy and years later had returned as a member of staff. There was no record at the publishers of this event and they were no longer looking for this kind of material.

Health issues intervened once more, and heart surgery for an aortic valve replacement was planned, when the Lord guided me to move into a retirement development rather earlier than I had anticipated. This determined that I had to do something with the manuscript, now in book format of just under 117,000 words. Along with Alan's large photographic collection of life in the exciting therapeutic and educational community that was Finchden, I committed it to the Planned Environmental Therapy Trust Archive, which became known as MB3. I was glad to assign the copyright to the Trust as a way of possibly supporting the care of all the documents.

By the time I had settled in my new home, my heart had deteriorated to the extent that I praised God for His timing and was glad to move forward through successful surgery. Recovery took a while, during which I was able to think further and pray, remembering the advice I had been given in ACW about the importance of sharing what you had written. Contact with Keith White through Social Work Christian Fellowship's fiftieth anniversary led to his offer to read the manuscript. I hadn't realised that he was on the editorial board of *The Therapeutic Care Journal*, an online publication of the MB3. They offered to publish the book online, through Amazon.

Throughout this long journey, from scattered notes to online publication, ACW members have encouraged, stimulated, given practical advice, taught me about the importance of a writing community, and kept me writing material for myself, as well as working on Alan's book. My regret is that making his publication known, planned as an event at a therapeutic child care conference in April 2020, was overtaken by coronavirus. But the book is still out there, available for Kindle or other tablet readers, *A Finchden Experience*, by Alan Wendelken, edited by Claire Wendelken Ross. Following surgery, I fell in love and married again at the age of seventy-seven, after twenty years as a widow. This has delayed any blogging and marketing ploys. However, all the readers' comments on Alan's book have been favourable. I just need to encourage social media 'likes'.

Claire Wendelken was called to social work when she became a Christian. After twenty-five years working in social services in a London borough, twenty years a social work tutor at Royal Holloway, University of London, and editing Social Work Christian Fellowship conference papers, she was delighted to finally complete, in 2019, the editing of her late husband's book on residential social work in a therapeutic community. She married Phil Ross in 2017 to become Claire Ross.

Birds on a Roof: My ACW Journey

Deborah Jenkins

From my bed, nursing an early cuppa, I watch birds on the neighbours' roof. They live behind a nature reserve and all sorts of birds gather there to watch and sing and welcome God's workmanship. Some stand out with bright colours and distinctive plumage – blue tits or great spotted woodpeckers. Others are less noticeable – pigeons or blackbirds. Occasionally, a heron sweeps down on majestic wings.

Sometimes, I imagine the birds are angels. While I sip tea and pray about the day, I fancy I can hear their conversation as they look across the close:

'Did you hear Larry at Number 10 lost that court case?'

'I know. But he's been praying a lot more since. I'm rooting for him!'

'Deborah at Number 18 has been praying more too, since that email.'

'Yep, I saw. How can we help her on her next step, do you think?'

What has this to do with ACW, I hear you ask? Bear with.

I became aware of ACW towards the end of 2005. Recently returned from nine years abroad, in Turkey, I was recovering from a debilitating condition which had threatened to steal my eyesight. It was (literally) a dark and frightening time. We had to return suddenly for treatment along with a teenager and a younger child who had never lived in the UK. Neither of us had work.

But we had a church, friends and a house, in London, which had been rented out while we were abroad. What helped me most, though my eyesight was draining away and the prospect of long-term recovery uncertain, was writing. I had written creatively since I was a child and in Turkey had discovered a group of writers all connected with an international church. I had started a small writers' group to read, encourage and comment on each other's writing. I did my first writers' course, with another English friend, in Istanbul.

This was led by an enthusiastic Antipodean who had been living in India. She had a vision to encourage writers in countries where their voices were unheard. There was a wonderful mix of nationalities on the course – Turks, Americans, Armenians, an Indian, a Belgian and we two Englishwomen. I cannot begin to describe the joy of writing in a rooftop apartment near the Bosphorus, a gleaming strip of water hemmed with palaces and minarets, the extraordinary Istanbul skyline. Gazing at that view, I wrote a short story which went on to be my first published piece. I knew then I needed two things to write well – community and beauty.

Back in London, teaching again, while undergoing treatment, and surrounded by cement, I had neither. I began to despair. But around the corner lived a fellow church member who was in ACW. We had been friends for a while but mainly by email. This friend invited me to an ACW meeting. I agreed to go but was full of trepidation. I felt an imposter, a one-eyed pretender who loved to write but didn't really feel she could call herself a *writer*. Surely a *real* writer had to meet the following criteria:

- Be published, several times, to loud acclaim;
- Feel proficient at her craft;
- Be paid to write.

I was none of these.

The event took place in a church building in the middle of London. The room was large and a bit gloomy, if I'm honest, but was soon lightened by the welcoming atmosphere. There was a bookshop, rows of chairs, a projector screen and good coffee. Best of all, the people were friendly and warm, of different ages and at different stages in their writing. This immediately made me relax. I can't remember who the speaker was, but it must have been someone inspiring because I remember feeling as though I'd left the intruder at the door. Much to my surprise, I felt I belonged here. Somebody I met told me she had been a writer for many years but 'hadn't been published yet'.

I remember thinking, 'Well, I am a writer, then!'

I left that day feeling motivated to try different types of writing, to be daring, to take risks. On the way home, I prayed and asked God to show me what He wanted me to write. I decided to join ACW.

After that, a number of things happened. Another local friend, also in ACW, asked if I'd like to write primary school textbooks. She worked for Macmillan and they were looking for writers for Social Studies textbooks for schools in the Caribbean. This was a great way of combining teaching and writing. Macmillan took me on, and I've worked for them, on and off, ever since. Through another ACW friend I began to write for the *Times Educational Supplement* (*TES*), who now commission me regularly to write for them. I started a blog. I also started writing for the ACW blog, More than Writers.

Then, with local friends, I started a writers' group which later became part of ACW, and through the encouragement and support of those writers, I self-published a novella, *The Evenness of Things*, on Amazon Kindle. Most of this was written at a retreat house run by another ACW member. I started writing devotional notes for CWR and even had an article published in the *Guardian* magazine about my eye condition, which had mercifully been halted. I had a travel article and a short story accepted for publication.

I continued to attend ACW writers' days in London and Birmingham and then in 2016 I went to a writers' weekend at

Scargill House, in Yorkshire, hosted by Adrian Plass, ACW's president, and his wife Bridget. There I met several ACW friends and made many more. I lapped up the worship and teaching, which addressed many issues related to faith and writing: what is a Christian writer? What are the different routes to publication? How do I know what God wants me to write?

What can be said about this beautiful Christian retreat centre? Perched on a rise between hills in the stunning Yorkshire Dales, the buildings, long and low, lie shouldered together like cats. They are grey, white and brown, surrounded by trees, and contain a chapel and a garden, walled with rose-coloured bricks. I have been every year since. I had found my beauty.

More recently, during the COVID-19 lockdowns, I've valued (daily) interactions with ACW friends via the Facebook page, and now have two little online ACW writing groups offering each other encouragement, prayer and Zoom chats. I finished my novel during the first lockdown, details for which were checked with one ACW member (a senior police officer) and edited by another (a professional proofreader). Yet a third agreed to be one of several beta readers.

This is another great thing about ACW people. God brings them from all walks of life. They want to serve Him and His people. They are helpers, sharers, champions of others.

Some do this in obvious ways (editors, publishers, an agent); others more quietly (posting the daily blog piece, sharing advice or time).

Like birds on a roof, they come in different shapes and colours. Occasionally, someone will be published, sweeping down with majestic wings. And here's the thing: they're cheered on; they're celebrated; their publications are read and shared. Not by everyone – we accept our different tastes and interests – but by enough of us to hold them high while they're up, and to offer wisdom when they come down again.

We're not perfect. There are disagreements, strong opinions. We are human, after all. But, held together by faith and words, our passions are for the same things: God and writing.

By lunchtime, the birds have gone, but this evening they'll be back. And their voices will join with songs on other rooftops, praising God for what He's done today.

It seems to me that we, in ACW, are like them.

For there are many ways to watch and sing, and welcome God's workmanship…

Deborah Jenkins is a writer of textbooks, educational articles and a novella, The Evenness of Things. *Her novel,* Braver, *will be published in the summer of 2022 by Fairlight Books.*

On the Fringe

Eirene Palmer

I'm suffering from something of an imposter syndrome writing this piece. I mean – Christian writer! *Moi?* Much of my journey has felt the equivalent of Saul on the road to Damascus but without the blinding light. More of a slow burn, I'd say.

You see, I fell out with God a long time ago. As many do. And it took me a very long time to understand that the God I kept at arm's length deserved to be there. A God with a long pointy finger and a loud shouty voice, rather than a loving God who would wrap His arms around me and offer me a large white handkerchief to dry my tears.

I had to change my image of God.

I was widowed in my early thirties. My young priest husband succumbed to a horrible disease despite the fact that a congregation of bishops and half the reverends in the country were praying for him. I was left homeless and hopeless with two tiny children and a letter from the church authorities requesting that I quit the parish. The new incumbent might feel threatened by me, apparently. I was up to my eyes in nappies, Calpol and Biff and Chip and felt no threat to a passing spider, much less a parish of 20,000 souls. In fact, a week after I buried my husband, the vicarage was invaded by a colony of bats. They burrowed, Hitchcock-fashion, down the cavity walls and pushed their way through the air vents at the bottom to come tumbling into the kitchen – thirty or forty one day while I cooked the kids' tea. I waited patiently for the bat people who were slow on the uptake but rapturous once they arrived at such a find.

God seemed light years away. Any well-meaning Christian who piously told me that it was 'God's will' or 'He's in a better place' was mentally chopped up into small pieces and put out for the birds. I am house-trained, though, and managed to smile sweetly and say nothing.

Fast-forward twenty or so years. I had raised the kids, worked, felt desperately lonely, went to church, sang in the choir. The stroppy side of me would say that it was only because I had good mates there, but the amiable side knows that deep, deep down where the sun doesn't shine, there was a kernel of yearning, of longing, of reaching out to hold and be held by something or someone who may or may not have been God. See! I wasn't giving anything away.

Then I fell in with a wise and experienced priest and we embarked on weekly conversations. She introduced me to a different God – one who was loving and kind and gentle. One who wanted the very best for me and, most of all, didn't want me to be scared. One who wasn't interested in my achieving some unattainable goal, but just wanted me to relax and enjoy being connected.

Get in!

At about the same time, I began worshipping at our cathedral church and encountered a depth of expression I didn't know was possible. The symbol, the ritual, the ceremony, so derided in the church of my childhood days, became sources of delight and contemplation. I joined the choir and began to pray as I sang.

I was being renewed.

I started to write.

Now, I've always been able to write. In my junior school, I won the Cadbury's essay competition every year and went home clutching a certificate and armfuls of chocolate. The other kids hated me. They thought it was a set-up! But as I grew older and there were no chocolatey incentives, I gave up. I had nothing to write about. Because, you see, when I write – when anyone writes – they reveal something of themselves, and I was painfully aware that I was sitting on top of a whole keg of desperation that I really didn't want to trigger with words.

So I stayed quiet. Until I began to talk and that was no longer an option.

That is when writing began to save me. After every meeting with my priest, I would head to my keyboard and pour out all my angst, my hurt, my pain on to the page. I would go back the next week and sometimes we would read it together, sometimes I would read it to her and sometimes it was all too much and I would chuck it in her direction as I headed for the door. But gradually, in the way that real healing is, something was working at a profound level, beyond my understanding or control, and I began to realise that the disapproving and critical God I believed in wasn't God at all.

I wanted to explore who a different God might be.

Now, most writers want to be read. We hunch over our laptops tap-tapping away and wonder if we'll ever win the Booker Prize. So I began sending off my musings to various publications. I started with the local parish magazine. The first offering popped through my letterbox on the night of the opening of the 2012 Olympics and I was so overcome by my new-found fame that I missed the Queen jumping out of the helicopter. I just couldn't believe someone had printed my words.

I graduated to publication in my cathedral magazine, which was a tad more – shall we say – steady, but had a much larger circulation. I had a regular spot in the local newspaper. I gained confidence and found myself published nationally for BRF's *Quiet Spaces*, in *Woman Alive* magazine and in two ACW compilations. I had no particular formula for this – I just 'sent it up', as my old dad used to say.

I had one rule: I would only ever write what felt authentic for me. I wouldn't be anyone else. I wouldn't try to pretend. The feedback I began to get was that people outside the Church appreciated my writing. I bumped into folk in the supermarket. We would chat among the frozen veg and they would tell me how my words had resonated and how they had been terrorised by early messages about hell and damnation and had abandoned church as a result. I realised that Vine Deloria Junior had it about right when he said, 'Religion is for those who are afraid of going to hell. Spirituality is for those who have already been there.'[32]

I decided that I wrote for those who were spiritual – which is everyone – even if they don't recognise it. Especially the people who don't go to church. The people who want to believe in God but are on the fringes, outside, looking in, as I was for so many years. The people who want to discover a God who loves them and won't throw them into a fiery furnace for letting slip a 'damn' or for not turning up on a Sunday without a sick note signed in triplicate.

Writing became my *raison d'être*. Then my second husband, Richard, and I began the Derby Cathedral Café Writers' group in 2017, affiliated to the ACW. I think my God has a great sense of humour because not only has She held and nurtured me all the way to a relationship with Her, She also helped me to realise that identifying as a 'Christian' writer doesn't mean squeezing myself into a little preordained box where I find it impossible to breathe.

I am a writer. I am a Christian writer. But being a Christian writer doesn't mean you only write for Christians. I write both for myself, to exorcise the fundamentalist demons of my childhood, and for others, to offer an alternative perspective, hope maybe, for all those alienated by a damaging theology of certainty. My writing journey reflects my spiritual journey. They are one and the same.

But mostly I am a writer who wants to share the good news of how much God loves every bit of Her creation.

---

[32] Vine Deloria Junior, www.goodreads.com/author/show/6729028.Vine_Delo ria_Jr_ (accessed 22nd March 2021).

I am discovering another God. An expansive God. A God who throws Her head back and laughs. A reliable God. One who will put Her arms around me and give me a big hug just when I need it. One who also loves my writing and encourages me to more.

As my very favourite saint, St Francis, said, 'I have been all things unholy. If God can work through me, he can work through anyone.'[33]

Eirene Palmer writes for those on the fringes of faith, outside looking in, and blogs at backstreetpilgrim.com.

---

[33] Cited in Cliff Garvey, 'If God Can Work through Me…', The Assisi Project, assisiproject.com/2020/07/23/if-god-can-work-through-me (accessed 10th March 2021).

Discovering My Niche

Janet Hancock

I joined the ACW in 2001. For several years, I had been attending the annual Winchester Writers' Conference. That year, my eye was caught by the ACW table.

I had started writing with a London School of Journalism correspondence course on short stories. I subsequently wrote a Mills & Boon romance, thinking – wrongly – it would be a stepping stone between a short story and a novel. Not that I'd read any Mills & Boon – not my sort of book. When I think back to my naivety bordering on arrogance in those early days, I still catch my breath. I also researched and drafted two historical novels and was planning a third.

After I started writing, I came to personal faith as opposed to knowing about the Bible: I'd been brought up to go to church, had studied Scripture for O and A Level and as part of my teacher training and BEd – at a Methodist college – and had taught Scripture to O Level for a few years. Coming to faith in the 1990s was not a Damascus Road moment, but rather a steering of this ocean liner on to a new course, toppling me off the throne of my life and installing the Lord Jesus. Writing, however, was something I kept for myself: I hadn't given it to God. From the 2001 Winchester Conference, I took home ACW membership details, hoping for direction, and help in keeping my young Christian roots watered and nourished. I found there was a regional group, Wessex Christian Writers, which met a couple of miles from where I lived. I also joined a postal group.

Meeting and praying with writers in the Wessex group one morning a month and circulating my work among the postal group enabled me to give my writing to the Lord, to pray about what I was or should be writing and what to do with what I'd written.

Once or twice a year, the Wessex group would choose six words at random with the task of incorporating them into a piece of writing: prose, poetry, an article, letter… I always wrote a short story. Over a few years, I wrote a dozen. The words 'gold', 'snow', 'rusty', 'holistic', 'biscuit', 'firecracker' developed into the 1,600-word story *New*, which told of a beauty therapist opening a salon above a Chinese takeaway. This won second prize in the Balsall Writers Short Story Competition and publication on its website.

'Gorgonzola', 'unexpectedly', 'lights', 'ecstatic', 'heather', 'daffodils' resulted in *Homecoming*, a 1,700-word tale of two seventeen-year-olds who fall in love but can't be together until years later when she has worked in Africa and he is in prison for GBH. This was placed second in the Yeovil Literary Prize and was published in its anthology. Most of my short stories were shortlisted or prize-winners in competitions and published in anthologies or online. A tutor at the Winchester Conference had suggested I enter competitions. I was developing a more literary style and learning about editing.

I returned to the first historical novel I had drafted years previously. I entered the First Three Pages of a Novel competition at Winchester and was thrilled to win first prize. Partials of the novel were shortlisted for the Yeovil Literary Prize and longlisted in the Mslexia Novel Competition. There was still work to do, but these encouragements drove me on to pursue publication. ACW friends in the Wessex and postal groups read chapters, partials and, in a few cases, the complete manuscript, giving encouragement and constructive – sometimes challenging – criticism, everything I needed to grow as a writer. After six drafts and three changes of title, *Beyond the Samovar* was published in 2019 by independent publisher The Conrad Press.

Many of my Christian friends don't read fiction; travel books, yes, and biography or memoir. There seems to be the feeling that if it's made up, it's not for us. I have struggled with and prayed about whether I should be writing fiction that is not specifically Christian. Yet, historical fiction can fill the gaps in what is known. For example, people may be aware that the Russian revolution took place just over a century ago followed by a civil war from which the Bolsheviks (Communists) emerged victorious. However, how might it have been for ordinary people living through the aftermath of world war and revolution? *Beyond the Samovar* takes place over a twelve-month period during 1919–20. The protagonists, a young English couple, are fictional yet rooted in their time and place. With their baby, they trek 2,000 miles across the length of Russia to a ship to England, although only two of them complete the journey. The reader can feel, 'Yes, this is how it must have been; what might have I done in that situation?'

My faith informed the writing of the book in terms of language used. I suspect that one of the reasons some Christians avoid fiction is because of the proliferation of offensive language. Some of the characters in *Beyond the Samovar* are rough, desperate people who can see no further than their own survival. In portraying them, I used all the senses: Russian feet bound with rags and bits of old tyre, people's smell, the feel of rough, calloused hands, how their voices sound. The reader gets the picture without my falling back on obscenities or blasphemy.

People a century ago faced the same issues we do about life, death and faith. Loss and horrors witnessed in Russia undermine the faith of Livvy, one of the protagonists in *Beyond the Samovar*. She can no longer pray or go to church. She confides this to Eleanor, who nurses her through scarlet fever:

Before it all happened, I used to talk to God: when things were difficult, or something I wanted. I felt, somehow, He was there. I don't now. I blame Him for allowing it.

Eleanor has had her own trauma:

For some time after Edward was killed, I was the same as you. If you want God to be there again, He will be. We are the ones who move away.

Thomas has lost three sons and his wife. When Livvy tells him about the massacre of Armenians, it is in an argument:

'They used to go to the Armenian Cathedral in Baku every Saturday evening. What good did it do them?'

'Livvy, faith is not an insurance against bad things happening.'

'So what's the point?'

'It is belief that in spite of terrible evil, good will prevail.'

Later, Thomas tells her of his crisis of faith after the death of his second son:

'I abandoned God in my despair but found that was worse than doubting God, raging why? Yet hanging on if only by the fingertips.'

Fiction can explore life's big questions, matters on which a Christian writer has something to say. Livvy finds the beginning of acceptance of a past she cannot change, an easing of guilt, an ability to focus on good. The start of healing.

I have received much encouragement along my writing journey and it's ongoing. I want to encourage other writers, whatever stage they are at. Keep going. Pray, take time to discover what sort of writer you are, what you really wish to write. Don't be shoehorned into something that isn't you. There may be times when writing is difficult or just not possible: in my case, bereavements, moving house, having builders and decorators in – not all close together, fortunately. Each time, a day came, perhaps after months, when I felt able to sit down and return to the work in progress, with fresh eyes and renewed assurance of God's unchanging love, grace and blessing.

This meditation on Psalm 23 was written in 2013 at a meeting of the Wessex group.

> Who else do I need when I have You? You sift through everything I say or think I want, and give me all that is right for that day.
>
> Be still, You say, and know that I am God.[34] And I draw breath, and know. Take time, You say, to step aside and be with Me. Take time to be. In the busyness and noise, listen for My voice and you will know the way to go.
>
> However hard the path, however bad the pain, I know that You are there with me, that You are already there when I reach that point. Help me, Lord, to remember this, to seek Your face, Your light in the dark times. You spread before me more than I could have imagined, blessings without number. Every day this is true, in this life and the next.

Janet Hancock lives in Dorset, where she enjoys choral singing and cultivating her courtyard garden.

---

[34] See Psalm 46:10.

A Writing Journey

Joan E Histon

The cool breeze blowing around my legs did nothing to improve my sour mood. I hitched my heavy bag bulging with sandwiches, papers, pens and laptop back on to my shoulder, stared down the empty railway track and gave a disgruntled sigh. It was 7.45am on a Saturday morning. I don't do Saturdays; I like my Saturdays at home, not waiting for trains on draughty platforms. I wasn't too keen on the topic I was going to hear, either. It was on playwriting – and I don't write plays!

I told myself I didn't *have* to go. Nobody has to do anything if they don't want to, I argued. Although who I was arguing with, I'm not sure. But then I was reminded that the only reason I had dragged myself out of my warm, cosy bed and was standing on the railway platform on this bleak Saturday morning was a growing lack of confidence in my writing. Why that should happen, I had no idea. I had been a ghostwriter for three Christian books published in the last ten years and they had all sold pretty well. That thought alone should have filled me with confidence. But it didn't.

My problem was that I had felt an urge to write something completely different; something that wasn't Christian-based, would reach a secular audience, but would have a trace of Christianity about it. The plot of having a Roman senator investigate Pontius Pilate a year after the crucifixion of Christ had totally captured my imagination. So, after much prayer, I went with it.

I was delighted with the finished result. I had loved the research element of *The Senator's Assignment*. I had fallen passionately in love with my Roman hero and had thoroughly enjoyed writing a historical thriller instead of being a ghostwriter. But the setback was, this book did not fit into my previous publisher's genre so had been rejected. I was devastated. Had I made a drastic mistake? I'm not a historian, and my historical thriller was so completely different from ghostwriting that it had left me unsure of my own artistry. So, and not for the first time in my writing career, I found myself praying desperately for guidance. That was why a nudge from God for this timely visit north to attend this meeting of the Association of Christian Writers had me standing on a draughty platform.

What I hadn't expected was a condescending nasal announcement through the railway public address system from some female who sounded suspiciously as though she was laughing at me: 'The 8.05 train to Newcastle upon Tyne has been cancelled due to industrial action.'

I hesitated briefly, but with a struggle decided that to go back home to my warm bed now would be taking a defeatist attitude. So, gritting my teeth and inhaling deeply, I legged it uphill to the bus station.

What I found to be so right about that whole ACW day was talking to other authors, listening to the uncertainties over their work, their successes, their trials and tribulations over finding a publisher, and their despondency over rejection slips. I soon began to realise I wasn't the only one who needed help along the way.

I had a long talk with one particular ACW member, a Scottish lady with a far greater insight into the world of writing than I had.

'No harm in being flexible with your writing,' she told me. 'Experiment, try anything, everything; see what works for you.'

That was a real confirmation booster. Yes! Changing genre was certainly working for me, I decided. I felt I couldn't leave without buying her book on marketing – which I did – purely out of politeness.

Another ACW committee member, with a good listening ear, suggested a particular publisher who might be interested in my novel. Duly encouraged, as soon as I returned home I sent *The Senator's Assignment* off to them. To my delight it was accepted and launched at the end of 2018.

The exciting follow-up was that the publishers liked it so much they requested a sequel. So, on 24th March 2020, *The Senator's Darkest Days* was launched. Yes – 24th March 2020. Remember it? The day of national lockdown for COVID-19. Excitement turned to despair as all my speaking engagements and book signings were cancelled, and the bookshops closed.

However, not all was lost. I suddenly remembered the book I had bought and the sound advice I'd received from the Scottish lady at the ACW writers' day a couple of years earlier.

'It's vital that as many people as possible know who you are and what you've written,' she had said.

The lady was called Wendy H Jones, and her book was *Power Packed Book Marketing*. Although I hadn't been interested in book marketing at the time and had put it straight on my bookshelf, with COVID-19 running riot I now had no option but to find a new source for marketing. So I dusted off the book, hungrily devoured the contents, began building new platforms and then launched myself on the unsuspecting social media scene.

Another suggestion that came from that day was joining an ACW local group.

'But you haven't any groups up north,' I moaned looking at their map. 'You're all southerners.' (With the exception of my Scottish lady, I hasten to add, and no offence to southerners.) But poring over the map when I arrived home, I noticed a group in Carlisle, about forty miles west from me.

I couldn't have wished for an easier drive. Thanks to the Romans, this straight road across the Pennines led me directly to the house of an ACW group in Carlisle. What a lovely band of warm people! We share our latest stories, writing problems, reading books and we pray together. I've spent many a pleasant afternoon in their company.

Am I glad I ran up the hill from the railway station to the bus station? You bet I am! I've come to realise we're not really alone when we write, are we? God gave us each other to help along the way.

Joan E Histon is a ghostwriter of three Christian books and the author of the historical thriller series, The Senator.

COVID, Courage and Contagion!

Margaret Jude

Cast your mind back to March 2020, and to the wave of fear and bewilderment that swept across our land and across the world. Coronavirus had struck. Lockdown was declared. Shops, businesses, restaurants and pubs were closed. Sports and leisure facilities were empty. All places of worship were shut. *We shut the church!* Streets lay empty as we stayed at home, worked from home, shopped online from home if we could, and life as we knew it disappeared before our eyes. We were in shock and disbelief, and any thoughts towards creative writing were definitely off my radar. But then…

Towards the end of that first week of lockdown, my husband and I sat down to watch television one evening as a distraction. We immersed ourselves in a wildlife programme called *Super Powered Eagles* (BBC) and were amazed at these beautiful birds and their capabilities. Something stirred in the back of my mind that I had heard about eagles many years ago, and a train of thought began to emerge. Energised, the next day I plucked up the courage to hit the keyboard, and created an article intended to inspire hope and encouragement. I emailed it to an elder of our church who held the database of all church members' email addresses, and suggested that, if he felt it was good enough, he could email it to everyone as a 'Thought for the Day'. He did so, and the reaction was electric, contagious and totally unexpected! It inspired others to begin writing their own 'Thought for the Day', and suddenly messages of hope, inspiration, encouragement and humour began pouring in. For weeks and weeks, hardly a day went by without a 'Thought' from someone, including some items from outside our own church, and it carried us through the chaos around us, through spring and Easter, and into the summer of 2020 and the eventual easing of that first lockdown, when we crept out, blinking like hedgehogs hauling themselves out of hibernation.

I felt that all these gems were too good to be lost as deleted emails, and suggested that we should compile them into a booklet, mainly so that our members who were not on email could read them. That idea mushroomed and, with a lot of help from others who had editing, copyright and publishing experience, the eventual outcome was a twenty-eight page, A4-size booklet of inspiring articles, illustrated with photos, and with a 'Picture Gallery' at the end demonstrating what our children and adults alike had been doing artistically during lockdown, including Easter Gardens and rainbows galore! We called it *Songs in a Strange Land*, based on Psalm 137:4: 'How shall we sing the LORD's song in a strange land?' (KJV). We had 100 copies professionally printed with glossy covers by a local printer, not intending it to be sold commercially, but mainly to be distributed among our own church friends and family, just asking for donations to cover the cost of printing. We also gave copies away free to our elderly non-computer members, who appreciated it so much. It was very well received by many, but most of all it was such a source of encouragement to all of us to look up, keep our eyes fixed on God and live in faith and hope through the darkness of the pandemic. We also now have a historical document to put in the church archives for future generations to see how our particular church coped during these difficult times. All this from one little message from the eagles!

When I set out to write that first tentative article, I had no idea where it would lead, what God had in mind beyond my writing, or what eruption of writing talent and inspiration would be unleashed! But I'm so glad I heard His prompting, and wrote it! I am also very grateful for the support of my local Cambridge

Christian Writers' Group, for their encouragement over the past few years to share my writings, and for introducing me to ACW, who published the very first article I submitted – much to my amazement! This lockdown experience has shown me that you never know where your writing might lead, how exciting your journey might be or how many lives might be enriched because of it. My advice to anyone reading this, who might be hesitant about their own writing? If God has placed it on your heart to write, then write! If you write, then share it. If you don't already belong to a group of likeminded enthusiastic writers, then join one. Above all, listen to God's prompting, and follow where He leads.

Below is the 'eagle' article. I hope it might inspire more people on their journey through whatever dark times they may be experiencing.

Thought for the Day
March 2020
Soaring Like Eagles[35]
Yesterday evening, we watched a programme on the television about eagles. It was called *Super Powered Eagles* for good reason! They truly are magnificent birds, with many unique features that enable them to be the absolute masters of the skies, with the ability to fly higher and soar longer than any other bird.

One of their special features not mentioned in the programme is their flight feathers. Obviously it is the amazing design of these feathers that enables such surpassing flying ability. But what makes them particularly special is that the eagle moults the older, worn-out feathers in a wave pattern, not losing all the flight feathers at once, which would seriously impede their ability to fly. Instead, as they are shed in waves, new feathers emerge in waves, so that the flight mechanism

---

[35] Edited for use in this book.

is constantly being renewed and replenished, so the eagle maintains maximum flying efficiency. Brilliant design? Brilliant Designer!

No wonder Isaiah chose the eagle as the example for his inspiring words, in chapter 40 verses 29-31:

He gives strength to the weary
and increases the power of the weak.
Even youths grow tired and weary,
and young men stumble and fall;
but those who hope in the LORD
will renew their strength.
They will soar on wings like eagles;
they will run and not grow weary,
they will walk and not be faint.

God does not totally discard or throw away the weary or worn out, either physically or spiritually. He constantly renews them! Isaiah goes on in chapter 42 to prophesy of Jesus, 'my servant, whom I uphold', saying, 'a bruised reed he will not break, and a dimly burning wick he will not quench; he will faithfully bring forth justice. He will not fail or be discouraged till he has established justice in the earth' (Isaiah 42:1, 3-4, RSV). God is gentle with us, He does not give up on us, He is able to renew us, constantly, and to use even us in His ongoing work of bringing justice and healing to this earth.

What an encouragement in our present situation! Maybe we are all bewildered, perplexed, anxious, and perhaps tired already with coping with the circumstances of isolation, inability to shop or do anything normally, and observing social distancing that goes entirely against our natural instincts. And then there is the natural fear of the threat of the virus, and all the unknowns. But God has designed us, as for the eagle, to be stronger than we think we are, with the ability to go beyond ourselves, with resources within ourselves that can be renewed and restored and strengthened time and time again, so that we do indeed soar on wings like *Super Powered Eagles*, empowered by His Spirit, at peace with God's sovereignty, filled with the knowledge of His love and grace, and His abiding faithfulness.

For the best summing-up of this message, we could do no better than to read the words of the much-loved song: 'Lord, I Come to You', written by Geoff Bullock, which is totally about the all-renewing power of the love of God. I recommend it to you.

Margaret Jude is an elder at Histon Baptist Church and a member of the Cambridge Christian Writers' Group.

Tales of Rwanda

Mary Weeks Millard

My writing career began late in my life and, from a human point of view, by accident!

When I was fifty-nine, my husband died after twenty-three years of coping with a neurological illness. Most of those years I was able to look after our three children and work part-time in nursing, but gave this up to look after Phil full-time for the last few years of his life. They were not easy years, but I discovered that writing poetry was a wonderful way of expressing my innermost thoughts and feelings.

A year after his death, in 2001, I was invited to be part of a small mission team going to Rwanda, to look at the needs and see how best they might be addressed. During that visit we were privileged to have a young Ugandan lad called Kabanda visit us and tell us his amazing story and testimony. After hearing it, one of the leaders of our team suggested that I might write Kabanda's biography. I do not know what prompted that suggestion, apart from the Holy Spirit, as no one knew that I had written a little book of poetry. I talked to Kabanda that evening and he confirmed that he would like his story to be written down, so we exchanged email addresses and left it that he would contact me when he felt ready to tell it in full.

Four years passed and I heard nothing. Meanwhile, I was busy continuing with short-term mission projects in Rwanda and almost forgot about the suggestion, until one night I woke up and it seemed as if the Lord was telling me it was time to write Kabanda's story. The very next day I had an email from Kabanda saying that God had told him it was time to contact me. With no experience and no one to help, I set about working by email with Kabanda to make notes on the details of his life up to that point.

Then I flew up to Scotland to secrete myself away in my brother's study and wrote the book in three weeks. On my return to Bath, the manager of the local Christian bookshop told me about a local guy who owned a small publishing company, who agreed to publish the book. It was ready for release in 2006 and I had just remarried and was on my honeymoon!

One of the people who requested a copy was the Anglican Archbishop of Rwanda, the Right Reverend Emmanuel Kolini. Having read it he then contacted me, asking if I would write the story of one of his ministers who had suffered greatly during the Rwandan genocide in 1994, yet from his experiences had developed a wonderful ministry of reconciliation.

I felt so inadequate when I was asked to do this, but I had met the pastor several times when I was working in Rwanda. I knew it would be a challenge as Rev Stephen Gahigi could not speak English and I would have to go over to Rwanda and work with him through an interpreter. My husband wasn't free to come with me as he had a parish to look after, so with huge trepidation I went to Rwanda for two weeks, and lived alone in a mission house. I worked each morning and afternoon with Stephen and his interpreter. The story of what he endured through the genocide was so horrific that I found I could not relax in the evenings or sleep at night. After a couple of days, I cried out to the Lord to help me.

I was sitting at the table with my laptop open in front of me, ready to play some music, when suddenly in my mind was a story for children about Rwanda. I wrote the first chapter – it was 'given' to me. When I finished that, I went to bed and slept well! The next evening, the second chapter 'came' – and so it continued throughout the time I was there.

I had no thought of publishing the story, but had enjoyed writing it. Once I was home, I wrote a second story, just for the fun of it. Those two stories stayed on my computer for a year or so. Meanwhile, my husband retired and we moved to Weymouth.

One day, I saw an advert on the noticeboard in the church we had joined, inviting people who were interested in creative writing to a Christian writers' group, held in the home of Joy Piper, who belonged to one of the other churches in Weymouth.

Like many writers, I am quite shy, but plucked up courage to contact her and went along. I received such a warm welcome and although I didn't really consider myself a 'proper' writer, I found the group helpful and encouraging. I decided to join ACW at once. I had no idea how important that decision was to prove!

A month or so later, my first magazine arrived. I read it from cover to cover and was drawn to a small piece of writing by a new publisher. She was asking for stories with Christian content of around 25,000 words suitable for children aged eight to twelve years. I thought of the two stories on my computer and looked at them again. They both met the criteria, so I sent them off. I received an acknowledgement and was told they would be considered.

A month or so passed and my husband and I went on a three-week mission trip to Burundi. Most of the time we were away from any internet connection, but one day when we had returned to the capital and the guest house, I was asked if I wanted to send any emails. When I opened my account there was an email from Dernier Publishing saying both of my stories had been accepted!

I remember the joy of that day! There was a realisation for me that maybe this was a gifting from God, and I should pursue it. With the encouragement of Janet at Dernier Publishing and my ACW group, I have continued to write and now have a new ministry, writing Christian fiction for children and young adults.

Here in Weymouth, our ACW group has held two writers' days, and at one of them, Janet Wilson, the founder of Dernier Publishing, was kind enough to come and speak about writing for young people. Our group grew in numbers after that day conference, so the meeting is now hosted at my home as we have a spacious living room and plenty of parking outside. The meetings help us to hone our writing skills, encourage and pray for each other. I am so grateful to belong to ACW – without it, I doubt that I would have become an established author.

Mary Weeks Millard is a retired nurse/midwife, who began writing in her sixties, and now at almost eighty years of age she still loves writing Christian fiction for youngsters.

How it All Began for Me

Michael Gowen

'Have you thought of joining the Association of Christian Writers?' my friend asked, as we came round to speaking about the book I was struggling to write.

'The what?' I replied.

'Association of Christian Writers. I think they have a Midlands group. I'll send you details of their website.'

That was how my love affair with ACW began. My friend is a writer too. He writes sketches, the type that can be performed during a church service, and they are very good. Ironically, he himself has never joined ACW.

He was as good as his word. So, armed with the information that he sent me, I had a look at the ACW website and found that there was a regular quarterly meeting of a group in the West Midlands, less than half an hour's drive from my home. The ACW subscription was minimal so, I reasoned, even if it proved to be a waste of time I would have lost very little. I signed up and was accepted into membership.

Very soon, a couple of the *Christian Writer* magazines arrived through my letterbox; and from the moment I started reading them, I was hooked. I discovered in them all the doubts and questions that I was musing over. Was I just writing rubbish? Would anybody ever want to read it? Was I wasting my time? Yet some of the people openly expressing these doubts were accomplished authors who had published books! What a relief! I was not the only one writing who had these doubts. What a comfort to realise that ACW was made up of people who could sympathise with me, even though many of them were much further ahead in their writing journey.

I decided to attend my first meeting of the ACW West Midlands group. Even though I had received a warm, welcoming email from the group convenor, it was with a mixture of anticipation and trepidation that I approached the door of the house in the suburbs of Leamington Spa. I felt very much the new kid on the block, both in terms of membership and of writing experience.

I need not have worried. Yes, some of the people present had numerous volumes in print. Some had even written bestsellers and been shortlisted for international awards. But others, like me, were still struggling with their first literary composition, and some were not even entirely sure why they were writing or what they wanted to write.

The acceptance of me within the group was immediate. As far as they were concerned, the fact that I was writing qualified me as a writer. I had a go at the exercise set for us during the meeting. When I came to read out my attempt and it was favourably received, my confidence was boosted. Perhaps my writing was worth something after all!

So much has happened since that first meeting, and it is hard to believe that it was only eighteen months ago. Even though we only meet once a quarter, bonds of fellowship and friendship have begun to form. I have been fascinated to see the range of different subjects that the members are writing about, and the diversity of literary forms. But, most of all, I have valued the acceptance of my own writing and the advice and help I have received.

The group members have taught me so much about proofreaders, editors, beta readers, publishers, self-publishing, preparing a book for submission to a publisher. I was even put in touch with a literary agent, who gave me invaluable advice on the manuscript that I am writing. There are so many potential pitfalls that the group has helped me to avoid.

As the year 2020 dawned, I saw that ACW was holding a writers' day in Birmingham. I thought to myself, 'Well, I ought to make an effort to attend' – never having been to one before – 'as it's only a few miles from where I live.' So in March of that year I turned up at St Luke's in Great Colmore Street, Birmingham.

It was an excellent day, but the most significant part for me was sitting next to a particular lady on my table. She was living in a village next to where I was born, so there was an immediate link. But more than that, I was intrigued by her life story, by the book she had published, and by how she had managed to publish it. I bought a copy there and then.

I always have a list of books waiting to be read, so it took me several months to get round to her book. When I finally did, I could hardly put it down. In it, she tells the story of her own harrowing encounter with the British criminal justice system on behalf of her brother over a number of years. Both gripping and disturbing, it has challenged me to reconsider some of my attitudes.

Having finished the book, I wrote an email of appreciation to the publisher, asking if he could kindly pass it on to the author. I like to do this if I have really enjoyed a book, as our human nature seems to naturally find it easier to criticise than to encourage.

She wrote an email of thanks in return, and I was pleasantly surprised that she asked how my own manuscript was progressing. In the intervening months since the writers' day, it had advanced and was then almost ready for submission to a publisher – though at that stage I was only beginning to examine publishing options.

I explained this to her and she replied, 'Why don't you see if my publisher is interested? I've been very satisfied with him.' So I did. To my delight, he said that he was willing to have the manuscript evaluated. I recalled that I had often asked God about how to go about publishing my book and I had always felt Him saying, 'When the book is ready, I will find you a publisher.' And now, perhaps His promise was coming into being.

There are still many hurdles to overcome. Will the publisher like my book? Will he suggest drastic revisions to it? Will the terms he proposes to me be acceptable? Will anybody be interested in it once it is published?

Nevertheless, I am convinced that, without the help and advice of ACW members, I would never have got to this stage. I have definitely become an informal advocate for the organisation. Several of my friends are also writing, and I have urged all of them to join. 'You can get so much benefit from it,' I tell them. One of them has actually taken that step and become a member.

Over the fifty years of its existence, I wonder how many other novice writers like me have been given the support, encouragement and confidence by ACW that they needed to go into print. Having had their writing published, I wonder how many people have been uplifted, amused, challenged, gripped and encouraged by it. We will never know until that final day when the definitive books are opened. Then each of us will marvel at how God has used our humble literary offerings and we shall say a hearty 'thank you' to ACW.

Michael Gowen recently retired to England after working and being in church leadership for twenty-five years in Belgium. He is currently writing his first book, applying the book of Daniel to life today.

It Started with a Poem

Michael Limmer

At the time, almost twenty years ago, I believed I was on a journey. Then, thanks to one short poem, I found myself travelling in a direction I'd never expected to take.

My ambition – perhaps obsession – had been, from a very young age, to be a writer. From my teens, I wrote full-length mystery thrillers. In those days, the early 1970s, you just parcelled up your manuscript with a covering letter and return postage and sent it off on a wing and a prayer to publishers carefully selected from the pages of the *Writers' & Artists' Yearbook*. I'd wait until about the sixth rejection before giving up on that particular manuscript. I'd already be heavily involved with the next, anyway, and that was always going to be *the* one; and never was. Two years ago, we downsized to a retirement flat, and I had to clear our loft. All those old manuscripts went to recycling; but what a great job they'd done over the years as loft insulation.

Twenty years ago, mounting stress and an understanding wife had persuaded me to leave a career in bookselling, take a less demanding job with fewer hours and have more time to write. I responded with alacrity, self-publishing a Christian novel. It did fairly well but didn't set the literary world ablaze. During my bookselling years, I'd written a couple of Christian short stories and some poetry, which had been published in a now long-defunct magazine called *Triumph Herald*. It led to me concentrating more effort into writing for the Christian market and I was soon publishing regularly in *Areopagus*,[36] a small press Christian magazine, which is, happily, still thriving.

Then I had the idea that some of my Christian poems, one in particular, might take the format of an A6 laminated prayer card, such as are sold in their hundreds through church bookstalls and Christian bookshops. I'd not long become a member of ACW and got in touch with a member of the committee, who provided me with a list of companies that published prayer cards. It was a long and useful list and I contacted and got a response from most of the names on it. Even so, I hit a brick wall.

But help wasn't far away. I happened upon a quarterly small press magazine called *Dial 174*. It was edited by a Christian writer and publisher named Joseph Hemmings, who liked some of my ideas. I began to contribute regularly to the magazine. Fiction writing was still my main thrust and I asked Joseph if he'd publish a booklet of my Christian short stories. He offered to do this at a charity rate, provided I agreed to donate a percentage of my sales to charity. At my request, he suggested Tractors for Romania, a small Norfolk charity run by ladies from a Methodist chapel in the neighbouring village. Their aim was to raise money to buy a tractor for a home for street children in Romania, so that the owner and his helpers could grow crops in the fields behind the home. The ladies eventually raised enough money to buy two tractors.

Joseph published a total of three booklets for me, but his greatest contribution was to use my poems as laminated bookmarks and prayer cards. The first of these was *that* poem, mentioned above. It became the first of many to be used in this way. I started to sell them through my local Christian bookshop (they're still doing this, fifteen years on), and, at his own expense, Joseph printed a large batch of my cards and booklets for the charity to sell locally.

---

[36] www.areopagus.org.uk (accessed 8th March 2021).

In the fullness of time, I came upon two other Christian charities and began to donate to them – as I do now – all profits from the sales of my work. Tractors folded after a few years, handing over the reins to Child & Family Aid, which, three years ago, handed over to Support for Romania. As I write this, I've learned that the trustees of this latter charity are about to retire and are asking their supporters to send their donations to Romanian Ministries.[37] Sadly, Joseph Hemmings died in 2014 and I've felt bound, because of all the efforts he made on my behalf, to support a charity helping Romania, as that country meant so much to him.

Another project involved Christmas cards. Back in 2005, Joseph published several hundred to sell for charity, to which I and another writer contributed the poetical messages inside. That led me, the following year, to design and print my own Christmas cards.

Within a year, Joseph was suffering with rheumatoid arthritis. It became so bad that I agreed for him to send me the laminated sheets, each containing four bookmarks or prayer cards, which I'd cut out individually. This proved labour-intensive – and still does – but it was nothing compared to what was about to follow.

One evening in 2006, Joseph phoned to tell me that his arthritis was so bad that he was forced to abandon his publishing operation. 'So,' he said, 'it's over to you.' Those words have been resonating with me ever since! He made me a gift of his massive printer, then I was on my own. Booklets – my own and those of other writers – Christmas, Easter and other Christian greetings cards, bookmarks, prayer cards, calendars have all followed over the years. To date, I've sold and distributed 700 booklets and 15,000 Christian greetings cards. I haven't given up on the mystery thrillers, either, having self-published my fourth in 2019, each with a Christian message.

---

[37] www.romanianministries.org (accessed 22nd March 2021).

In all this, I firmly believe that God is leading me and has done so throughout this particular journey since that initial idea for a prayer card, which took a little time to get off the ground. Also, while I've been writing for charity, I've found new sales outlets through the many talks I've given to various fellowship groups about the charities I serve. As I adapt to changing circumstances, one door closes and another opens: our Lord is ever inventive and encouraging, showing us new paths to take.

I've also been conscious of the presence of ACW in all this. Over the years, I've been offered much sage advice, freely and generously given, concerning potential markets, and a wide vista of competitions. My main interest has been in Christian fiction. It's a dwindling percentage of the UK Christian market, which is strange, because our Lord was a storyteller. There may be few outlets, but ACW has often pointed me in the right direction for placing material.

There's also the feeling that, as a Christian writer in an increasingly and alarmingly secular world, with ACW behind you you're not alone, and it helps you to hang on to your integrity. We're all writers with the same aim in mind: to spread His timeless message and glorify His name through the written word.

Michael Limmer, a retired bookshop manager, is a writer of mystery thrillers, Christian fiction and poetry.

A Daring Struggle

Patrick Baker

I remember creating one of my first pieces of writing on an Easter House Party at Scargill House. I arrived for the weekend in a bad way. I'd been working for some time as a counsellor in a therapeutic community for adults with mental health problems. In this stressful situation, the cracks had been showing up in me too.

During the weekend, I attended a creative writing workshop. To aid our imagination, the chaplain who was leading it had made a simple display of a loaf of bread and wine. Taking my cue from this, I set out on a poem focused on the Last Supper. Into it, I poured my own anguish and brokenness: I was as much the fragmented bread as Jesus was. Several times I nearly gave up on what felt like a daring struggle, to be honest, but the leader encouraged me to keep going and I eventually wrestled the poem to a conclusion.

When she then asked me to read it out at one of the services, I felt naked as I stood up. But the poem made quite an impact and afterwards several people commented on how it had helped them. I have used the poem a few times since then and, years later, I happened to meet the chaplain again, now a vicar. Did she, I wondered, remember me and my poem? Yes, and she had used it in services she was leading.

The lesson I learned from that experience – and hope I have held to in my writing since – is to tell it like it is.

Breaking

First, I was a grain of corn.
Life was a breeze, a sun-bath,
A warm, dizzy dance on the waving stalk.
Jesus came by one day and I thought he might pick me
On his afternoon stroll
But he didn't.
Then came the cruel blade,
The sickle I could not escape.
I was cut, toppled, crushed, beaten, pulverised,
Ground away to nothing
By hands that didn't care.
I fell apart.
Then other hands began to put me together.
Picked up the pieces
And made something of me: a loaf of bread.
Smell me: Hovis, cobbles, childhood,
Life as it ought to be,
Rich and slow.
And then it began again.
The hands that took me away roughly,
Off the shelf, God knows where.
Just when I thought I had it all together.
Men gathered round me, hungry men who smelled of
fear.
And Jesus was there.
A different Jesus.
A mixture of joy and anguish I'd never seen before,
I'll swear his hands shook as they picked me up.
'This is my body,' he said.
And I wanted to say, 'I don't know, it feels more like
mine.'
But he was right.
It was his body.
And he knew what was going to happen to him,

What he was going to do.
He was going to walk right into it,
Lay himself down between the millstones,
And crack them for ever.
(Easter 1994)

Patrick Baker started out as a teacher and has 'careered' through life in a variety of different jobs and adventures which have resourced and enriched his writing life.

God's Timing

Richard Palmer

I sometimes wonder if there are clocks and calendars in heaven. I think I know the answer. But occasionally, I want to shout at God that I still haven't heard back regarding that impassioned prayer from three weeks ago. Nor have I had a reply to that urgent can't-wait request from this morning. Living in the age of social media and emails, we expect prompt responses. For instance, my Gmail account sends me a reminder after five days if I've not heard back from folks.

There seems to be a big disparity between heavenly and earthly time. I agree wholeheartedly with Pierre Teilhard de Chardin[38] when he says, 'We are not human beings having a spiritual experience. We are spiritual beings having a human experience.' Because we are stuck in this temporal and physical world, our outlook is predominantly time bound and materially focused. Is this where the wet gets in when it comes to God's timing? It could offer some explanation for the following story.

Back in the heady days of the turn of this century, I was a member of the Southwell Christian writers' group, The Inkjets, run by Penny Young. It had been a local writers' day in Nottingham that had originally drawn me into the Fellowship of Christian Writers. I ended up running the group for a couple of years and got a tremendous amount from the group and the

---

[38] Although it is widely believed the quote originated with Pierre Teilhard de Chardin, this is disputed.

experience. Here was my first entrée into ACW, as we later became known.

Fast-forward ten years and I moved to Derbyshire. There was no local group and my ACW membership had lapsed. I had a vague notion that I might think about starting a local group someday. But I didn't.

Then I did. It was becoming clearer to me that a big part of my writing ministry was to encourage and help others in their writing journey. After seven years in Derbyshire, the idea of a local group re-emerged from this. In 2017, my wife and I were early retired, doing quite a lot of writing and coming across a few colleagues who were doing the same. Why not start something? Within a couple of weeks, we had a quorum of six interested parties, took the plunge and organised an exploratory meeting.

It was a bit like putting breadcrumbs out for the birds. The initial small group tweeted their find to others and soon a bustling flock appeared from nowhere and we founded Café Writers, based at Derby Cathedral. It's amazing how many writers are out there, sitting in the trees, waiting for some encouragement to come out into the open.

Now in our fifth year, we are blessed with a large group of wonderful people. Why did it suddenly seem right after all that time to start a group? Don't ask, it just did. I'd love to tell you of angelic visitations in my dreams, of demotivated writers knocking on our door, begging us for help on their writing journey, and weeping poets, desperate to woo a willing audience with their heartfelt lines. No, it was none of that. It just felt right. But that is not the only mystery of God's timing on this journey. There is more.

A certain Mary Mills was in that original Inkjet group. Both she and Penny Young have since been to our Café Writers meetings and have led presentations for us, a happy reconnection from earlier ACW days. When the fiftieth anniversary of ACW first reared its head, I was talking with them about what history they had on the subject. Many of us were starting to root around in attics and ferret about in the back of old filing cabinets, unearthing dusty or slightly damp items of ACW memorabilia.

It was the end of 2020 when Mary emailed me. She had been with Meg Jones, leader of the National Forest group, who had given her a copy of *Candle & Keyboard*, the predecessor to *Christian Writer*, from May 2003, containing an article of Mary's, entitled, 'Prophets without Profits?' (She was our non-commercial writers' coordinator at the time.) She said something about a letter of hers as well. I read the article and skimmed through other pages. There was her letter on the letters page, and beside it was another letter that caught my eye. It opened by saying, 'Am I alone in feeling a certain isolation in the provinces? It is so good to see Events Days being organised by ACW but do we have to go all the way to London to attend? … Can't we have a few more regional days? There is life west of Guildford and north of Watford.' This correspondent was clearly having a bit of a rant.

Here was a letter close to my own heart. It went on to bemoan the lack of connection between national and local groups and the lack of coordination between our local groups. 'In the 15 months that I have coordinated the local group, the only contact I have had is with the Editor of *Candle & Keyboard*,' it went on. 'Isn't there an opportunity here to work more effectively as an Association, spreading our best practices between the groups, between local and national levels learning from one another, supporting one another and becoming a bit more purposeful and meaningful in what we are about?' The letter writer was getting a bit heated, but I liked what the person was saying. Imagine my shock when I got to the end of the letter to see the signature of Richard Palmer. What? It was from me! No wonder I liked its sentiments. I had absolutely no memory of this letter. I had not read Mary's email properly, and had missed her pointing out that there was a letter from *me* in there as well.

The editor's response was the icing on the cake. 'More connections between regional groups is an excellent idea, one which the Areas Groups' Coordinator may well help to organise. At the moment, I'm holding the fort as AGC and would be happy to receive any ideas such as Richard suggests.' I never heard any more about it.

Yes, but who was the groups' coordinator now? Oh, that would be me. Hmm, a God with not only a perfect sense of timing, but also a sense of humour. Eighteen years after my letter, in essence a prayer, appeared in the May 2003 edition of *Candle & Keyboard*, the idea had come back to me: with force and with conviction, because now I had the means and the will to enact it. And the coincidence was that I had been saying that I was going to organise a get-together of our local group leaders to network on our thoughts and ideas.

Why, I mused, had no one done this before? The answer was simple. It only really becomes practical now that so many of us have become Zoom-savvy through pandemic decree. Our local group leaders are scattered liberally and widely across the UK. Only now do we have the means and will to meet together and network online to share all our good ideas and experiences.

Eighteen years! It's a long time to wait for answers, which arrived through a very convoluted route of people and experiences over many years to bring me to a place where I could in fact bring some closure to my frustrated prayer within that letter.

As writers, our patience is important because the hopes and dreams we harbour for publication, national or local, can often be a long time coming. Often, the rejection slips are so demotivating. But then, as in my story, some encouragement may appear from unexpected sources via unexpected means at unexpected times. Julia Cameron talks of this in *The Artist's Way* (Souvenir Press, 2020): 'We tend to believe we must go out and shake a few trees to make things happen. I would not deny that shaking a few trees is good for us. In fact, I believe it is a necessity. I call it *doing the footwork*. I want to say, however, that while the footwork is necessary, I have seldom seen it pay off in a linear fashion. It seems to work more like we shake the apple tree and the universe delivers oranges.' So true. And well worth remembering in our writing journeys.

God's timing, always perfect. Sounds like I'd better get on with it.

Richard Palmer is ACW's groups coordinator and is currently enjoying writing on the spiritual journey and the human condition.

World on Fire

Sharon Heaton

I crested the summit of the dunes and paused, somewhat surprised. A scene of unexpected destruction lay before me. Second World War army trucks, Red Cross ambulances, rowing boats and boxes of munitions were scattered carelessly across the golden beach. I dug in my walking boots, sugary grains of sand shifting away in front of me, as I cautiously approached the shoreline.

However, all was not what it seemed to be. The vehicles and boats were real enough, but the distant tanks were little more than plywood cut-outs, the abandoned Citroën car a useless, empty shell. The noisy thrum of generators and the snake-like coil of electricity cables completed the stage set. Lytham St Annes' beach, now known as 'wartime Dunkirk', had been taken over by a film crew. Filming of the BBC drama series, *World on Fire*, had begun.

Out of the corner of my eye I caught sight of an enormous German shepherd dog bearing down on me and froze instinctively as the cold, wet muzzle of the powerful animal touched my hand. The dog trainer called Samson back. He slinked off — wolf-like, yet obedient — a star in his own right. I breathed freely once more.

I was fascinated, having undertaken months of research trying to get to grips with the escalating tensions on the Swiss–German border prior to the Second World War, in order to create my own wartime tale. I had lovingly created characters, placing them in dangerous and often bewildering situations. My intention today was to quietly contemplate the storyline, to commune with God and seek His guidance on a deserted beach. Instead, I was surrounded by a dramatic reconstruction set in the era of my novel. God works in mysterious ways.

This unforeseen encounter inspired me: the smell of smoke and taste of fear, the juddering din of the 1930s petrol engines, and the raw energy of it all. The riveting re-enactment was an assault on the senses. More importantly, where was God in all of this unfolding drama? The director could cut and pause filming. I might step away from the keyboard to contemplate my own plot. But what did God do? Was He merely a silent observer?

My hand rested on the latch of the church door. It was late September in 2019 and I was about to enter a world that was new to me — one occupied by ACW writers and poets. What would they be like, these Christian writers?

Val, the leader, greeted me warmly. She began by introducing me to the rest of the group. Tim, a Cornishman by birth, but an honorary Lancastrian by marriage, had penned a poem, which is now engraved into the glass-panelled entrance of Preston Railway Station. I know because I have seen it. James is also a prize-winning poet. Dame Judi Dench gave a performance reading of one of his verses. Shirley, a longstanding ACW member and former group leader, writes witty, insightful short stories and poetry, mainly about her native Lancashire and the Fylde coast. Julie had recently received a critique of her novel. I had just submitted my own completed Second World War manuscript for review, too.

We shared our experiences. Val modestly omitted to tell me that she is a published author, journalist and Christian broadcaster, herself.

There was a buzz of excitement about the meeting. It was the launch of *The Blessing Diaries: Musings to Sweeten the Soul.* Everyone had submitted something: poems, short stories and prose. Members were asked to read aloud their contributions from the crisp pages of the newly published volume. For many, it was the first time they had held the completed work in their hands. I felt truly blessed to have shared the precious moment.

Val's husband, Bob, sang a plaintive song about a young man returning home after wandering abroad as a stranger. I had spent the previous week revising my novel and wrestling with a similar theme. What would such a reunion be like, especially as there was acrimony at the outset? Tears welled in my eyes as I suddenly realised that the young man's homecoming in the song was to heaven, itself, rather than to some earthly home. God was present in that moment.

I next attended the ACW writers' group in early December, eager to see my new writing friends. Val asked us about our recent writing exploits. I felt sufficiently confident on this occasion to share my piece of prose entitled, 'World on Fire'.

Tim had brought copies of his *Poetry Diary for 2020*, containing his own beautiful verses, one for each month of the year. A happy photo of a sun-drenched beach adorned the cover. We enthusiastically planned the ACW meeting schedule for the coming months. I decided to write the dates out neatly in my new diary, courtesy of Tim. The pristine pages were filled with burgeoning hope for the year ahead.

Val set a task for us all: 'I want you to write a piece on the theme of "home", any style, any genre. What does home mean to you? I'd love to read what you've written when we next meet in March.'

I decided to take a different route home at the end of the meeting. The sun was beginning to set behind the grass-clad slag heaps, creating a glistening red glow on the window panes of the tightly huddled terraced houses. The road was unfamiliar to me and, quite unexpectedly, I found myself driving past the Pentecostal church I had occasionally attended as a child. Long-lost memories were stirred. The lines of an old hymn by Harry

Tee sprang to mind, and I sang the chorus of 'They Were Gathered' fervently, from the bubble of my car.

The planned meeting in March did not take place, of course, for we were all in lockdown, but the writing continued.

I crested the summit of the sand dunes, my eyes scanning the horizon. The beach lay before me, a rippling golden carpet. There were the usual dogs haring about with their owners and a lone kite surfer was catching the waves, but little more. It was as if the bustling activity and explosive power of the previous week had never occurred. I felt a bit let down, left like an abandoned child. Where had they all gone?

My novel would soon be completed. Already the main character was striding away into the distance, and I experienced the pang of loss, like that of losing an old friend. Then, as I headed out aimlessly across the sands, I noticed something — nothing. No scorched earth from the bombing, no flotsam and jetsam of debris washed up on the shoreline — everything was as it should be. Well done, production crew, for leaving behind a pristine beach after *World on Fire*.

As we wander through this life, our footprints are stamped into the rifts and rills of the path we choose to tread, only to be quickly erased by the encroaching tide. We have been placed on this earth for a brief point in time. Our objective — to stir up the flame of fire that God has placed within us, using our gifts, talents and abilities for His glory. Ultimately, when the 'wood, hay, [and] stubble' (1 Corinthians 3:12, KJV) have been burned up, what is left is refiner's gold.

Sometimes, the Holy Spirit can so ignite a poem, short story or novel, that it becomes a living flame, licking up the pages with words that have been wafted into existence from the throne of God Himself. There is a life to the words, and a liveliness, like that of a flickering flame. Those are moments to be cherished. May the flame of Pentecost so ignite our work that it glorifies God and is used for His kingdom. May the Lord renew us by His Spirit, so that Christ may shine through our writing and set the world on fire for Him.

Sharon Heaton is an enthusiastic member of the Mancs and Lancs Christian Writers' Group and is hoping to have her first historical novel published.

A Write Life

Sheelagh Aston

The phone call came one Friday in early February 2019. The day I acquired a sense of my mortality. My plans for engaging in retail therapy evaporated as I learned of my ex-husband's unexpected death. He had no family living in the UK apart from our two grown-up children, so I arranged the funeral and put his chaotic affairs in order. Out of the frenzy of activity came the feeling of life whizzing past me at fifty-something. I had so many questions to answer. What did I really want out of life? What did I not want to look back on and regret I had not done? Time and time again one answer emerged – writing.

I wrote as a child and continued throughout my adolescence into adulthood until work, marriage and children arrived. Several years later, while going through a messy divorce and adjustment to single parenthood, the solace of writing resulted in a self-published young adult novel in 2008. Good reviews came, but the demands of a full-time job and teenage children meant it slid down the list of priorities on my time.

Jump to late 2018, two years after settling into my present post, the old familiar nudge prodded me, accompanied by vivid, technicolour dreams telling the story of characters formed from the dust particles of my imagination. It made me ask the question that had bothered me over the years. Maybe now, anchored in calmer waters and both children getting on with their own lives, it would not be selfish to devote time to writing? Writing did seem a self-indulgent occupation. I would be the only beneficiary. It didn't bring anyone to God – unless they were attending a service where I used one of my meditations. I was not sure whether it was God or me who wanted it as part of my life. The question did not leave me and neither did the familiar pang of how I missed diving into the challenge of plotting, characterisation and narrative description.

One evening, a few weeks after the funeral, still dealing with the estate and two traumatised offspring who were experiencing their first brush with death, I found myself at my computer, a blank page on the screen and my hands poised over the keyboard. Letting my mind connect with my imagination, I began to tap-tap. Two hours later and 700 words in, I went to bed and slept like a felled log.

Over the next three months, I wrote every day, usually at night. Only my son, who lived with me, knew what I was up to. I searched for a local writers' group to no avail. At my son's suggestion, I went online and found a Christian writers' group whose members were from all over the world. With a pen name and photo of my dog as my motif, I found myself with those who understood the quirky nature of wanting to write. Ability ranged from writers like me, beavering away when other commitments allowed, to full-time traditional and self-published authors. Most amazing for me, they wanted to share and help each other. A secure critique forum allowed members to post extracts of their work and in return provided feedback on other members' material.

The criticism, even with the negatives, was honest, constructive and encouraging. In forums, I learned different plotting approaches, methods to develop believable characters mixed in with sharing the joys and tribulations of finishing that tricky scene and how to persevere when writer's block jams transmission from your creative hub. Most of all, I had found a spiritual home where writing had a place. God had led many members to write and, later, with the ACW UK group, I found myself able to let go of the doubt that my writing was an indulgence. It had a valued place in my life; for what purpose, I had yet to discover.

I could discuss all-things-writing without the embarrassment of the glazed look or perplexed comment from those who knew me – not that I told anyone, and my son was sworn to secrecy.

Feeling very out of my depth, I offered what I hoped was helpful feedback, to find my comments endorsed by more-experienced writers. Maybe I was not completely barking in my decision to take writing seriously? There was still one acid test I needed to take: having my own work critiqued.

My fingers shook as I pressed the 'submit' button for my first post. Having explained I was dyslexic, the comments focused on the story, plot and narrative with several 'good catches', ie, observations on head-hopping, disembodied limbs and turns of phrase.

Five months and several drafts later, I had my novel ready, but was it any good? The online site had a forum with posts arranging beta reading of each other's work. I knew I needed a complete stranger with a sharp pen and trigger-happy finger on the delete key to tell me whether it held any signs of credible writing. I had not written for several years and had no publishing track record to speak of.

I sent my manuscript to the same literary consultancy I had used for critiquing my young adult manuscript. (The assessor back then had ripped the YA novel to shreds before providing advice on how to stick it back together for the better.) Off went my precious manuscript, with all my fears. I waited six weeks and kept an eye on my email inbox in trepidation for the assessor's report. The fact that this time the assessor lectured on an MA creative writing course, wrote historical biographies and freelanced as an editor did not fill me with much hope of coming away scar free.

I glossed over the accompanying email with its 'hope you find this helps' spiel, downloaded the report and clicked to open it, closing my eyes.

They were polite – 'Thank you for sharing XYZ …' Perhaps they would be gentler this time? '… which I read with great page-turning interest in a single sitting.' By the end of the first paragraph, I was yelling for my son to tear himself away from his own computer screen and look at mine.

For hours, I kept returning to the hard copy to reread the report I had printed out. I devoured all the positives and noted the constructive suggestions among them to improve it. More precious than gold, the report gave me the assurance that I was not writing in vain. The time and energy spent to create the story had produced something worth more than scrap paper.

OK, I had a way to go. I did one more draft to bring one of the two protagonists into the story earlier, but it was worth the effort. Worth it because someone who didn't know me but knew about the craft of writing saw something in my scribbling. They had understood the story and its complexities and thought it good enough to encourage me to carry on writing.

Over a year has passed. I continue to write and to share with my online writing family. My confidence has grown, leading me to join ACW in 2020. I took advantage of lockdown to write, though I still did not share with anyone other than my children what I was doing. With nothing published, no stamp of approval, it seemed pointless. Late one evening in the autumn, I thought, 'Why not?' and submitted a short story, 'Going Home', to the ACW magazine. Several rejections from agents and publishers over the novel had pulled apart my confidence like a stitch unpicker. I found myself questioning why I had started to write again in the first place. After eighteen months, I had a box file with three manuscripts and a fourth in the computer – destination nowhere. Perhaps I should just accept it was simply a hobby, something to keep me sane during the mad year of COVID-19 and fill the quiet evenings. 'Be satisfied you have something that gives you pleasure,' I told myself.

One late December morning, I received my copy of the ACW's winter magazine. Over cornflakes, I flipped through the first few pages. Printed on page 6, the chosen short story's title looked oddly familiar: 'Going Home'. I opened my mouth to say to my son that it had the same title as my short story, when I noticed the author's name: mine. My name in print! The ACW magazine may not be the *Times Literary Supplement* or one of the festive stories commissioned by the *Church Times*, but it didn't matter. The whoevers that produced the magazine had seen fit to publish my story. A Booker Prize moment, if ever there was one!

One family WhatsApp and work tweet later, I had gone public on my writing. The response that came was with good wishes and interest in reading the story. Maybe I am not so odd after all. Maybe God had a plan. It has just taken me a while to understand what it is. Use what God gives. Don't hide it under a bushel.

Sheelagh Aston lives in the north-east of England and shares her time between writing, working as a vicar and being a mum.

The Ugly Duckling

Sue Cavill

I always wanted to be a writer, but it was only when I joined an ACW group that the penny finally dropped that I was one.

There were various clues along the way. As a five-year-old I won a writing competition in *The Church of England Newspaper* and it published my little account of my summer holiday in Margate. My prize was a book called *Rex and Mistigri*[39] and I still have it.

As I grew older, I enjoyed writing stories for school essays but also had my own projects, filling exercise books with adventures, sending stories and poems to the Puffin Club for its competitions. I was runner-up in another competition in *The Church of England Newspaper*, this time for a science fiction story about how the oceans became so polluted that there were no fish.

My enthusiasm for writing influenced my choice of degree and I studied English and Latin, with the aim of understanding more about how the great novelists and poets in both languages worked. I also felt that grappling with Latin grammar would help me to write grammatical English.

I had a clear idea of what sort of writer I wanted to be: a novelist. To me, publishing a novel was the holy grail. Only when I had done this could I call myself a writer. I was sure that when I did write a novel, my Christian faith would influence the

---

[39] Rene Guillot, *Rex and Mistigri* (London: The Bodley Head, 1963).

subject matter and the moral compass of my characters. In the meantime, in early adulthood I wrote short stories as assignments for a community creative writing class, and a couple of them were published in *Christian Woman* (now *Woman Alive*).

I was also able to use the writing skills I had developed so far in my work. My first job after graduating was with the Scout Association's official magazine, *Scouting*, and while there I wrote a few articles that were published with my by-line. The first time I saw my name in print was very exciting. Following that, I worked for a small PR agency which also published in-house newspapers. My job was to write and edit the house journal of a well-known pharmaceutical national. I was therefore writing to a deadline and to length for publication once a month. Even now, if someone asks me for 300 words on a subject, I can write something and, without counting the words, know that it will be pretty much the right length. But although I thought that at a stretch I could describe myself as a journalist, I did not really consider myself a writer. A writer writes novels.

Following the birth of my children, I had a part-time job putting together a prayer diary for a Christian mission organisation. I then had what I considered at the time to be my big break. I was commissioned by IVP to interview a number of people from different walks of life about their Christian faith. The interviews would be published in a book called *Talking Heads*. I thoroughly enjoyed travelling around the country meeting these interesting individuals and writing up the interviews. J John was the lead author of the book and he wrote the introduction and the conclusion, explaining faith to readers.

At last, although this was not a novel, I had written most of a book, published with my name on it, and I had been paid for it. I felt that this was the beginning of being a real writer. My next books might be non-fiction, but non-fiction authors were still writers. I started talking to various people about what my next project might be.

However, life intervened and I had to go back into full-time employment, which meant my plans for writing books were shelved. With two young children and a job, I didn't have the energy for additional writing projects.

Yet I was still writing. In my new job, I was a press officer for a learned and professional body, and in that role I was required to write press releases that summarised scientific research accurately, with a 'hook' to draw the reader in. My boss was very exacting and, after a while, I decided that he had made a pact with himself always to correct with his red pen at least one thing in every release I wrote. Even if they were good enough, he taught me that they could always be better. He also had a rule that, except in extremely rare circumstances, the releases should never be longer than one side of A4. Once again, my writing skills were refined as I kept to that rule.

In this job, I read all kinds of journalism to understand what sorts of stories would be interesting to what sorts of readers, and to slant the press releases accordingly. I learned that writers for *The Sun* newspaper are some of the most skilled journalists in the world, as they have perfected the art of encapsulating complex news into short, easily understood paragraphs. I learned how to explain the academic research we were promoting so that a non-specialist (such as myself) could understand it. As a Christian, I tried to make sure that whatever I wrote was truthful and wholesome.

I moved on to a job in communications with the NHS and for more than ten years I was responsible for helping to communicate NHS policies to various audiences. I decided that I could call myself a communications specialist. I was writing reports and documents and articles that were published in professional periodicals, but I still didn't define myself as a writer. Interestingly, by now my husband had published a large number of academic articles and books, together with popular books on his subject, and had also ghostwritten a number of Christian books. I felt that he was the family writer, rather than me.

Eventually, I took voluntary redundancy from my NHS role. I had recently moved to Derbyshire and was invited by a friend to join the Derby ACW group, Café Writers.

There I found a warm welcome, but I felt reticent. Was I a writer?

I talked with the group leader about my experience of writing media releases and how churches could publicise their activities by sending out releases. As a result I was asked to give a presentation to the group. In my talk I decided to go through some simple steps on how to write a media release (something I'd led training on in previous roles) and suggested examples of the sorts of news items that local media might be interested in. I talked about how I had sent out press releases to local media which resulted in publicity for my church's activities. I wanted to show the members of the group how they could use their writing skills to show the wider world what the Church was doing.

As I put my talk together, I had a light-bulb moment. Even though I hadn't written a novel, all the writing experience I had gained over the years, the refinement of my skills in my various jobs, meant that I was a writer. And I was a Christian writer, not just when I was writing about specifically Christian topics, but all the time.

I thought of the song 'The Ugly Duckling'. The ugly duckling thinks that he isn't a swan, because he doesn't recognise that swans are ugly ducklings first. Eventually he looks in a mirror and realises he is a swan.

Thanks to ACW's Café Writers group in Derby, I realised, 'I am a writer!'

Sue Cavill worked in PR, communications and public engagement for many years and now freelances using the skills she developed, while enjoying more time to explore her own interests in writing.

A Story Emerges from the Past

Vince Rockston

A chuckle, issuing from the cave I had thought abandoned, startled me. Then a deep voice boomed, *'Sic, vos tandem placuit venire ad me, filius meus?'*

Instead of taking the 'bird cage' lift, we had struggled up the zigzag path to the top of Monte Capanne. Surrounded by monstrous boulders and a few struggling pine trees, we enjoyed our picnic lunch. Several neighbouring islands and the Italian coast appeared in the misty distance. After trudging down a different way, our guide mentioned an ancient cave – 'Just up there!' – in which an exiled bishop had lived after fleeing the invading Lombards. Although by now we were all weary, something drew me up that steep path to the simple cave. And that's when I heard that chuckled call. My school Latin was rusty, but – 'Have you decided to come at last, my son?' – how could someone be expecting me?

Wherever I travel, I look for an authentic historical novel set in that location: *The Bridge Over the Drina* when in Sarajevo, Bosnia; *Tanausú: King of the Guanches* during our holiday in the Canary Isles, etc. But we were hiking on the Isle of Elba, and the only books I found in English were about Napoleon's brief time there. Hardly a local.

Could it be that San Cerbone (St Cerbonius) was calling me from a long-lost past: 'Why don't *you* write a book about my adventures with God?'

'What, me? I'm no novelist. I write technical manuals.'

But the impulse persisted and I began my research. I bought books on late antiquity, civilisation in the Middle Ages, clothes and crafts in Roman times, guide books about Elba, as well as contemporary writings such as Boethius' *The Consolation of Philosophy* and *The Letters of Cassiodorus*. Cerbonius turned out to have been a contemporary of St Benedict of Nursia. They may have met; at least, they had common friends – or should I say, enemies – such as the invading Ostrogoth King Totila. *Spoiler: A close colleague of Benedict, Placidus, sneaks in at the end of my book as the Abbot of the monastery on the neighbouring Isle of Capraia.*

A year after that initial incident, I made a follow-up visit to Elba to explore the sites and paths around where Cerbonius had lived. I was fortunate to meet up with some local specialists, who organised private viewings of two local museums housing historical artefacts, and answered many questions: Angelo Mazzei ('the only polyglot on Elba'); and father Paulo and son Silvestre Ferruzzi, both architects and authors of books on the history of the island. These two honoured me by interrupting their meticulous renovation work on the Madonna del Monte chapel, which is not far from Cerbonius' cave, to share their spaghetti lunch with me and hear about the book I planned to write.

Born of Christian parents in Carthage, North Africa, in AD 493, Cerbonius was ordained a priest by Bishop Regulus. Persecution by Arian Vandals caused the local Christian community to disperse and Cerbonius escaped to Italy. There he gained prominence when he was – reluctantly – appointed Bishop of Populonia, Tuscany, and had interesting encounters with sceptical Pope Vigilius. War raged as the Roman Empire crumbled, and Cerbonius took refuge in a cave on Elba, where many people still lived in pagan darkness. *Aquila* was beginning to form in my mind: my fictitious Silvanus – fascinated by nature but struggling with adolescent issues, family tensions and an overwhelming fear of the vengeful gods – meets up with the wise old hermit…

My intention was to use an unfamiliar age and setting to explore timeless issues facing young people: work and play, discovering one's unique talents, conflict with parents, the lure of ill-gotten wealth, sexual temptation and budding romance, the longing for adventure, the pointless cruelty of war. And, above all, spiritual questions: was it Zeus and the fearsome gods of the boulders and winds who made and rule the world, or Cerbonius' God, Jesus? Does God still speak and intervene in the world today? How can I be freed from the guilt of past misdeeds and find a purpose in life? What happens when I die?

I discovered the Association of Christian Writers: Christian authors seeking to encourage and learn from each other. Just what I needed. Their magazine *Christian Writer* included an announcement for an inspirational weekend at Scargill House with Adrian and Bridget Plass, long-time favourites of ours. Without much delay, my wife and I signed up. As it meant flying from Switzerland, we took the opportunity of hiring a car and visiting friends we hadn't seen for years.

Delightful lanes winding through the meadows and fells of Yorkshire brought us finally to our destination: a charming conference centre, radiant with love and faith. 'Panning for Gold', the theme of the weekend, turned out to be both immensely stimulating for us fledgling authors and a chance to meet many ACW regulars, as well as the inspiring broadcaster and author Sheridan Voysey. Since then I have found much fun and encouragement through ACW's lively Facebook group and enjoyed reading several members' publications.

I have attended a few writers' weekends in Zürich, with speakers such as the amazingly successful Joanna Penn, and joined a regular critique group for a couple of years, a practice I would highly recommend! ACW has local writers' groups throughout the UK. I've also found invaluable resources online, such as the very pertinent tips at helpingwritersbecomeauthors.com by K M Weiland ('a fighter, a writer, a child of God'), practical advice from the late John Yeoman, and many, many others.

And so *Aquila: Can Silvanus Escape That God?* began to take shape, slowly, tediously. Early feedback from friends made me aware I had very much to learn. What is a hook, a beat, an inciting event? How should I make use of cliffhangers? What's the difference between – and significance of – scenes and sequels? Show, don't tell! It's conflict that drives the story. Strong verbs avert the need for adverbs. Avoid unnecessary backstory and the sneaky 'As you know, Bob …' trope. Use foreshadowing cautiously. Kill your darlings!

Finally, I've also learned how important it is to employ professionals for editing (although it's painful to be told 'the book is fundamentally flawed'), for cover design, for proofreading, etc. That means being prepared to pay. (A good portal for such services is reedsy.com.)

Vince Rockston is the author of Aquila: Can Silvanus Escape That God? *(Grey Owl Books, 2019). A former physicist/IT consultant/technical writer, he is now enjoying retirement in Switzerland. He blogs at aquilaelba.info.*

Epilogue

Understanding Wells

Nicky Wilkinson

We need water to survive, but we need the Spirit to live. The well is the access point. Drinking deeply of the Spirit of God is critical to the living water flowing from us, our hearts and our pens.

The well has been a powerful motif for this compendium. Our hope at ACW is that you have been inspired and encouraged by the testimony of past and current ACW writers in digging and drawing from the well, and have been equipped further in priming the pump, your skills honed to reach higher levels of excellence.

In the Old Testament, Abraham had to contend for his well as we read in Genesis 21:25-30. He needed to be clear and decisive with his enemy. This well was called Beersheba, 'the well of the oath', because Abraham called on God to witness his dominion over the well before the Lord and his enemy. While our productivity grows, we too must fight for our wellspring of life.

In the New Testament, as Jesus met with the Canaanite woman at the well in John 4:1-45, He revealed His divinity to her. He challenged her to exchange an exhaustible supply for the eternal waters of life, inspiration and joy. At the well He revealed the truth about her identity, elucidating the limitations of her current lifestyle and thus recalibrating her destiny and pointing her beyond the temporal to the real issue of eternal satisfaction. As we meet at the well, we too can be refreshed, restored and redirected.

We are commanded in Scripture to sing to the well (Numbers 21:17), because our lives depend on it and its author. The well is from the hand of the One we sing to and celebrate. Here our identity clarifies: as we gaze into the reflection of the river of God, we see our image reflected in His gaze and our destiny can flow again with vigour. As the waters flow, our pen flows.

Prayer

Our Father in heaven, thank you for the gift of writing and the privilege of being connected to a fellowship of writers. As we gather at the well of Your Holy Spirit, fill us with Your presence to encourage and sustain us, Your passion to inspire us and enable us to inspire, and the priestly anointing to communicate what You put in our hearts.

Empower us to unleash the pen of a ready writer. Equip us with discernment and insight as we write. Guide us and help us safeguard the gift You have given us, to bring it to fruition.

We choose to forgive those who have impeded us; forgive us too where we have acted out of despair not faith. Heal us from the fears that distract us, and the rejection that dismays us. Give us strength, patience and endurance to keep going in all seasons. Help us to overcome the internal inhibitions and the external obstacles with process and technology. Deliver us from the forces that would block our access to You or prevent us from finishing the task.

For Yours, Lord, is the power, the glory and the majesty. We live to serve You and fulfil our destiny on earth. Amen.

Nicky Wilkinson has recently returned to the UK after spending eight years in the Czech Republic followed by eighteen years in Zimbabwe where she taught History. She is now the ACW administrator.